Thomas
Alva
Edison

Thomas Alva Edison

VINCENT BURANELLI

Silver Burdett Press
Englewood Cliffs, New Jersey

To Nan

PHOTOGRAPH ACKNOWLEDGMENTS:
Edison's Birthplace Museum, Milan, Ohio: p. 4–5; Firestone: frontispiece, p. 110;
General Electric Company, Schenectady, N.Y.: pp. 38, 48, 52–53, 64; From the
Collections of Henry Ford Museum & Greenfield Village: p. 15; U.S. Department of
the Interior, National Parks Service, Edison National Historic Site: pp. 2, 7, 11, 31,
62, 68, 80–81, 121.

SERIES AND COVER DESIGN:
R STUDIO T • Raúl Rodríguez and Rebecca Tachna.

ART DIRECTOR:
Carol Kuchta

MANAGING EDITOR
Nancy Furstinger

PROJECT EDITOR:
Richard G. Gallin

PHOTO RESEARCH:
Roberta Guerette, Omni-Photo Communications, Inc.

Library of Congress Cataloging-in-Publication Data

Buranelli, Vincent.
Thomas Edison / Vincent Buranelli.
p   cm. — (Pioneers in change)
Bibliography: p. 127
Includes Index.
Summary: A biography of the inventor who changed the world in which he lived
with such revolutionary inventions as the phonograph, electric lighting, and motion
pictures.   1. Edison Thomas A. (Thomas Alva), 1847–1931—Juvenile literature.   2.
Inventory—United States—Biography—Juvenile literature.   [1. Edison, Thomas A.
(Thomas Alva), 1847–1931.   2. Inventors.]   I. Title.   II Series.
TK140.E3B87M1989
621.3′092′4—dc19
[B]
[92]

89-6014
CIP
AC

CONTENTS

The Young Inventor

Thomas Alva Edison was once asked when he intended to retire. He replied, "The day before the funeral!" His prediction was a good one. As it turned out, he kept on working—thinking, writing, planning, experimenting—until he became too weak to continue, just before his death at the age of eighty-four. To the end of his life Edison was an example of his most famous saying: "Genius is one percent inspiration and ninety-nine percent perspiration."

Whenever Edison was called a genius, he was quick to point out that he could never have made his great inventions if he had not been a hard worker. For every experiment that succeeded, he carried out many that failed. He continued through repeated disappointments that would have made nearly anyone else give up.

He explained his stick-to-it attitude in this way: "Everything comes to him who hustles while he waits." Edison was

Samuel Edison, Jr., Thomas's father, moved to the United States from Canada in 1837.

always a hustler. That is one reason why he was able to change the world in which he lived with such revolutionary inventions as the phonograph, electric lighting, and motion pictures. He added ninety-nine percent perspiration to the one percent inspiration with which he was born, and became the world's greatest inventor.

How Thomas Alva Edison did it is the story of his life. His family was of Dutch and English origin. His great-grandfather came to America from Holland in the early eighteenth century. When the American Revolution broke out in 1776, the Edisons remained loyal to King George III. Refusing to accept American independence, they moved to Nova Scotia after the war.

However, Samuel Edison, Jr., Thomas Alva's father, became involved in a rebellion against the Canadian government. When the rebellion failed, he fled across the border into the United States. Samuel settled with his wife, the former Nancy Elliott, in Milan, Ohio. He worked as a sailor, a carpenter, and for a time as as innkeeper.

Samuel and Nancy Edison had seven children, four of whom survived past childhood. Thomas Alva, the youngest, was born on February 11, 1847.

He was a precocious child who took an interest in everything going on about him. In 1849 covered wagons began to pass through Milan carrying forty-niners on the first leg of their journey from the eastern states to the California gold fields. These covered wagons were called prairie schooners. Young as he was, Edison stood spellbound at the sight. "I had a great longing to climb into those prairie schooners," he said as he looked back years later, "just to see where they were going."

Young Edison's desire to find out about things some-

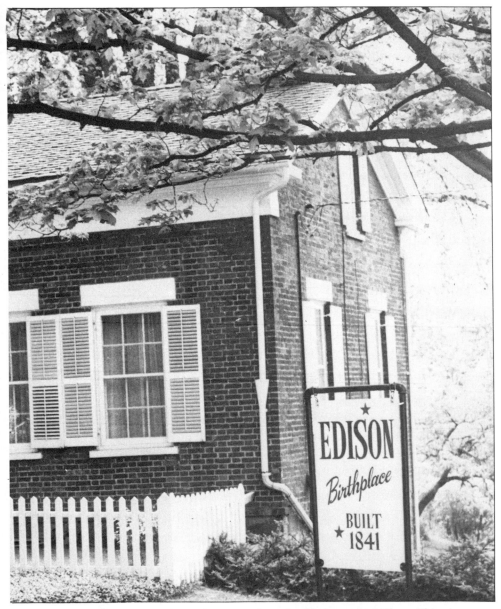

Thomas Alva Edison was born in this house in Milan, Ohio, in 1847. The Edison family moved to Michigan when Thomas was seven.

times got him into trouble. Once he thought he could hatch eggs by sitting on them. He naturally smashed the whole lot, with some damage to the seat of his pants. Bending over to inspect a bees' nest, he offered a target to a ram, which charged forward and butted him into a fence. He was unable to sit down easily for the next few days.

Fire fascinated him so much that he experimented with it in the family barn. One day the barn caught fire and burned down. To teach him a lesson, his father thrashed him in the town square.

Edison also was involved in a real tragedy. He went swimming in a canal with another boy who drowned. Too frightened to know what to do, Edison ran home and said nothing until questioned about the disappearance of his friend. The experience made him decide never to conceal the truth about anything that might be important to other people.

In 1854, when Edison was seven years old, the family moved to Port Huron, Michigan. There he attended school without much success. He always got the worst grades in the class. His quick mind was on things other than the three Rs—on the wonders of nature, for instance, and the pattern of the stars in the night sky.

His mother heard Thomas called "addled" by the teacher. So she took him out of school and taught him at home. Nancy Edison was qualified to do this because she had been a teacher before her marriage. Together she and her son went through English, history, mathematics, geography, and penmanship. They also read some classics of literature, among them Gibbon's *The History of the Decline and Fall of the Roman Empire*.

Reading great literature remained a habit with Edison.

Nancy Elliott Edison, Thomas's mother, had been a schoolteacher before she married Samuel in 1828, at the age of seventeen.

He realized that being taken from school and taught by his mother at home was one of the most fortunate things that ever happened to him. Referring to the fact that Nancy Edison always encouraged him to do his best, he said: "My mother was the making of me."

Edison was also close to his father, who, although a stern disciplinarian, taught him the virtue of hard work, thrift, and honesty. Samuel Edison kept a large vegetable garden. Thomas Alva and a friend, Michael Oates, took the produce to market. Each week the boys loaded a cart with potatoes, beans, peas, corn, tomatoes, and lettuce. Hitching a horse to the cart, they drove into the town. There they sold their cargo to Port Huron merchants or to passers-by who wanted fresh vegetables to take home.

When the last potato or bean sprout was gone, the boys drove the cart back to the Edison home. They turned the profits of their labor over to Nancy Edison. She paid Michael his wages, gave her son his allowance, and used the rest of the money to help meet the household expenses.

When he was about ten years old, Edison built a laboratory in the basement of the family house. Shelves against the walls held bottles containing as many chemicals as he could buy in Port Huron or find in the town dump. While experimenting with different chemical combinations to see what would happen, he often caused sharp, bad-smelling fumes to drift throughout the house. This made his mother threaten to put an end to his career as a chemist.

Edison soon shifted to experimenting with the tele-graph. Nancy Edison must have been pleased. Her son was now working in physics rather than chemistry.

The telegraph was a marvel of the nineteenth century. Its invention followed from the scientific experiments of

8

Michael Faraday, a British scientist. Faraday's work led to the development of a whole new field called electromagnetism.

Before Faraday's experiments, it was known that an electric battery could send an electric current through a wire. This discovery was made by an Italian scientist, Alessandro Volta (from whose name we get the English word *volt*). Volta's battery was not very useful in a practical sense. That was because his battery caused an "all or nothing" phenomenon. That is, when you turned it on, an electric current flowed through the wire. When you turned Volta's battery off, the current stopped. There was no way to make the current go on and off while the battery remained on.

This problem was solved with the discovery of the electromagnet. In 1820 a Danish scientist, Hans Oersted, discovered that if a wire is carrying an electric current it is surrounded by a magnetic field. Within a few years an English electrician, William Sturgeon, discovered that if a wire is wound in a coil around a good conductor of electricity (an iron bar, for instance) the current flowing through the wire causes the conductor to become a magnet.

Knowing that electricity could cause magnetism, Faraday experimented to see if magnetism could cause electricity. He proved that this is indeed the case. In 1831 he showed that a conductor moving into a magnetic field around a magnet became electrified. Moreover, if the magnet was turned, the conductor lost its electricity. The conductor regained its electricity when the magnet was turned back to its original position. Thus, by controlling the movements of the magnet, one could turn an electric current on and off as it flowed through a wire.

The ability to send electrical impulses in long or short bursts through magnetic control made the telegraph possible. A pattern of long and short bursts—dashes and dots—could be used to symbolize the letters of the alphabet.

In 1837 Samuel F.B. Morse exhibited his system of telegraphy. It consisted of a key that, when pressed down, broke the connection between a battery and its wire. Very brief depressions of the key produced a series of dots. On the other hand, longer depressions produced dashes. By grouping dots and dashes in a different pattern for each letter, a telegrapher could represent the entire alphabet. The Morse code became the universal method of sending messages by tapping out dots and dashes.

Edison became interested in the telegraph from watching the telegrapher at work in Port Huron. The children of the town used to hang around the telegraph office. They liked watching the telegrapher send out those mysterious dots and dashes by pressing his key. But young Thomas Alva Edison was the only one of them, as far as we know, to experiment with this remarkable method of communication.

Of course, he didn't make any great inventions at this time—that couldn't be expected of a boy not yet in his teens. He did not even know the Morse code. Nevertheless, he learned something about batteries and electrically charged wires. This was a lesson that would be very useful some years afterward when he took up the study of telegraphy in earnest.

His experiments in the basement of his house became less frequent after 1859 when he accepted a full-time job. He became a "candy butcher" on the Grand Trunk Railway linking Port Huron and Detroit.

Each morning he climbed aboard the baggage car of the train. There he filled a basket with candies, dried fruit, and other snacks, as well as newspapers. When the train pulled

Thomas Alva Edison at the age of fourteen. He had begun to work on the Grand Trunk Railway when he was twelve.

out of the Port Huron station, Edison walked up the aisle between the passengers, crying out his wares. He did the same on the return trip from Detroit to Port Huron.

One morning, when Edison was trying to climb onto the moving train, a trainman helped him aboard by grabbing him by his ears. He attributed his deafness to this incident: "I became deaf when I was about twelve years old. I had just got a job as a newsboy on the Grand Trunk Railway, and it is supposed that the injury which permanently deafened me was caused by my being lifted by the ears, from where I stood on the ground, into the baggage car. Earache came first, then a little deafness, and this deafness increased until at the theater I could hear only a few words now and then." He considered the trainman who pulled him aboard responsible for his loss of hearing. However, medical science suggests that a childhood illness may have been the main cause. He suffered from scarlet fever, which can cause deafness in later years.

In any case, Edison thought his hearing impairment actually helped him. Now he spent less time talking and more time reading. He became a great reader during the train's stopover in Detroit. What was he to do with those hours before he returned to Port Huron? He tells us: "My refuge was the Detroit Public Library. I started, it now seems to me, with the first book on the bottom shelf and went through the lot, one by one. I didn't read a few books, I read the library."

That feat would be impossible today. But the library was just beginning more than a century ago. The number of volumes on the shelves was so small that Edison could read them all. He could spend a few hours reading almost every day during the years he rode the train.

Edison recalled one trip between Port Huron and Detroit when the train jumped the tracks. Nobody was hurt. But the baggage car tipped over so far that the contents of his basket were thrown out. He saw candies and dried fruit strewn all over the tracks. Edison realized that there was no hope of selling them because of the dirt and soot into which they had fallen. However, he decided to save what he could and eat them on the spot.

The result did not do the young Edison's stomach any good. In fact, he became so sick that his mother called in the family doctor. Edison told the end of the story this way: "I gave our family doctor the time of his life." Edison survived and continued with his job on the train.

When the Civil War broke out, Edison was only fourteen. Although the conflict went on for four years, his increasing deafness made it impossible for him to volunteer for the armed forces.

News of Civil War battles reached Detroit by telegraph. Edison used this fact to his advantage in 1862 at the time of the Battle of Shiloh. He realized that people in the towns along the train routes would want to know what was happening at Shiloh. So he went to the *Detroit Free Press* and persuaded the editor to let him have one thousand copies of the newspaper. Then Edison sent telegraph messages to the stationmasters along the way. He asked them to post notices that when the train arrived newspapers would be on board giving full accounts of the battle.

Edison wrote of his scheme: "When I got to the first station on the run I found that the device had worked beyond my expectations. The platform literally was crowded with men and women anxious to buy newspapers. After one look at that crowd I raised the price from five cents to ten and sold as many papers as the crowd could absorb.

"At Mount Clemens, the next station, I raised the price from ten cents to fifteen. The advertising worked as well at all the other stations. By the time the train reached Port Huron I had advanced the price of the *Detroit Free Press* for that day to thirty-five cents per copy and everybody took one."

His experience on that particular day taught Edison a lesson: Quick-wittedness in taking advantage of opportunities is a key to success in life. He looked for opportunities after that. Rarely did he miss one he could profit from.

In that same year of 1862, he began to publish his own newspaper, the *Weekly Herald*. This was the first newspaper to be published aboard a moving train. Of course, it was not a "real" newspaper, nothing like the *Detroit Free Press*, only a single page printed on both sides. But it was an achievement for a boy of fifteen.

The idea for the *Weekly Herald* came to him when he considered that railroad workers, businessmen, and residents of the towns along the train routes would be interested in local news. The conductor allowed him to give his idea a try. So Edison bought a secondhand printing press in Detroit. He set it up in the baggage car of the train.

He became a reporter for his publication, gathering news items to be covered and writing about them. He also doubled as the editor, fitting these items into their proper places on the front and back of his sheet. And he served as his own printer. He set the type. He covered the letters with ink. Then he forced the plate down onto the paper to produce a printed page.

The contents of Edison's newspaper were remarkably varied. First, there were the announcements of the Grand

Trunk Railway. These included changes in timetables, reports on delays, and similar information. Stagecoaches met the trains in those days, just as taxis do today. Passengers getting off at a particular stop with a copy of the *Weekly Herald* knew when and where they could board the stage for their next destination. Entries under "Lost and Found" told readers about items from men's canes to ladies' jewelry that had been left aboard the train.

Business notices were important. The *Weekly Herald* carried advertisements from hotels, restaurants, and stagecoach lines. It listed the price of goods in the markets, from food to clothing.

Personal items included births, marriages, deaths, anniversaries, club meetings, and other events that advertisers wanted to make public.

Like all news editors, Edison sometimes found that there was not enough news to fill all the available space. When that was the case, he followed their example. He resorted to what are called "fillers" in the trade. These can be anything from sports records to biblical quotations. Edison often used proverbs or adages of the "waste not, want not" type.

Edison thus kept two jobs going aboard the train at the same time. But this was not all. He found time for a third interest. The young Edison maintained a laboratory in the baggage car. He set up the lab next to his printing press, copies of his newspaper, and his supply of snacks for the passengers.

The desire to experiment was becoming a passion with him. Being away from home most of the time, he could not work in the laboratory in his basement very often. He transferred most of the chemicals to the train. The conductor did not know what he was getting into when he agreed to let Edison conduct his experiments on board.

At first all went well. Whenever Edison had sold all his goods and had no printing to do, he devised experiments. Of course his chemicals did not smell any better than at home. But the wind blowing through the baggage car carried the fumes away. The conductor allowed the experiments to continue because none of the passengers ever complained to him.

The men who ran the train developed a high regard for the young experimenter in the baggage car. The engineer even allowed him to handle the controls between stops.

Then a disaster occurred. While Edison was testing phosphorus at his bench, the train gave a sudden lurch to one side. The phosphorus fell to the floor amid a pile of newspapers, which burst into flames. The fire spread. Dense smoke filled the car.

Desperately Edison tried to put the fire out. He pulled whatever might catch fire out of the way, stamped on the blazing papers, and swung his jacket at the flames feeding on the wood of his shelves. Nothing worked. The fire and the smoke increased.

Suddenly the conductor, having seen the cloud of smoke billowing from the baggage car, rushed in with pails of water kept aboard for an emergency. The conductor managed to put out the fire. At the Smith's Creek stop, he ordered Edison off the train. He tossed all Edison's belongings after him—laboratory equipment, printing press, copies of the *Weekly Herald* that had survived, and charred remnants of the candy butcher's basket.

The train vanished down the tracks while a forlorn Edison gathered his belongings. He was permitted to return to his job. But the conductor warned him that his experimenting days in the baggage car were over.

Those days had not been wasted. Edison had developed into a first-rate experimenter. He knew much about chemical formulas and the physical properties of matter. From his reading in the Detroit Public Library, he knew about recent inventions in telegraphy and photography. Self-trained, he was ready to become an inventor himself.

He took the first step toward independence in what might be called Edison's "Horatio Alger incident." In the late 1800s Horatio Alger's stories for boys were very popular. In Alger's stories the hero usually performed a good deed and was rewarded for it. Perhaps he stopped a runaway horse, with danger to his life, and found that the driver of the buggy was a bank president, who offered him a job as a reward.

Edison's "Horatio Alger incident" occurred at the Mount Clemens railroad station. He was returning to the train with some newspapers under his arm when he saw a young child run out onto the tracks in front of a moving boxcar. Dropping his papers, Edison raced onto the tracks. He grabbed the child and tumbled out of the way with him as the boxcar lumbered past.

The child turned out to be the son of the Mount Clemens telegrapher, J.U. Mackenzie. In gratitude, Mackenzie offered to teach the rescuer how telegraphy was used along the train routes. Edison eagerly accepted the offer. The telegrapher soon taught him everything he knew about the science of telegraphy. He taught him about the Morse code, whose signals were sent from one train station to another.

Edison learned how to warn stationmasters that trains

were coming through or were delayed. He was also able to tell them when accidents along the line meant that passengers had to take other routes. He mastered all the skills needed to send and receive messages.

Shortly afterward, Edison left his train job and struck out on his own as a professional telegrapher.

The Tramp Telegrapher

In 1863 Edison found a telegrapher's position in Port Huron, but a dispute with his employer cost him his job. He then went to Stratford Junction in Ontario, Canada. There he served as a railroad telegrapher on the night shift throughout 1864. He was the only one on duty during those hours. He was responsible for alerting stations up and down the lines about the passage of trains through Stratford Junction in both directions.

He was ordered by his superior to show he was awake on the job by sending a signal every half-hour to the nearest train dispatcher. However, only two trains were scheduled to come through Stratford Junction at night. Edison saw no point in staying awake and on guard during the rest of the time. He therefore attached a clock to the telegrapher's key in such a way that the key sounded the signal every half-hour—while he was asleep in his chair.

Unfortunately for him, a night came when the dispatcher, aware that the signal was sounding properly on the hour and the half-hour, decided to call back. The dispatcher, of course, received no answer. Alarmed about what the reason might be, he rushed to Stratford Junction. He found the telegrapher sound asleep and the key tapping out its messages automatically as the clock triggered its mechanism.

The dispatcher shook Edison awake and fired him on the spot. Edison found another job in another Canadian town, Sarnia. This time he stayed awake all night. Still, he missed a signal to hold a freight train to allow another train to pass on the same tracks in the opposite direction. Unknowingly, the freight train barreled right through Sarnia toward the incoming train. A tragic accident would have occurred. But the two engineers, seeing each other's headlights in the darkness pulled their locomotives to a stop in time to avoid collision.

Once again Edison was looking for a job. He returned to Port Huron only to realize, after long, hard searching, that telegraphers were not in demand there. Consequently, he became a "tramp telegrapher," wandering from place to place. He took temporary assignments wherever he could find them. In 1864 he worked in Adrian, Michigan; Fort Wayne, and Indianapolis. The following year he found work in Cincinnati, Nashville, and Memphis. In 1866 he was in Louisville and in 1867 in New Orleans.

Of all the American cities, Cincinnati impressed him the most. The metropolis on the Ohio River was enjoying an economic boom based on trade from the Mississippi, agriculture, and developing industries. Theaters and concert halls made Cincinnati a cultural center. Music from German immigrants contributed much to the culture.

Edison enjoyed the artistic side of Cincinnati. He and another telegrapher with similar tastes, Milton Adams, went to the theater together. William Shakespeare's *Othello* was one of the plays they saw. Music became Edison's favorite art. He heard old operas by Rossini and new operas by Verdi and Wagner. He developed a love of Beethoven that never left him. He always said: "Beethoven's greatest symphonies are the summit of human creativity."

In addition to working at telegraphy for a living, Edison also resumed his experimenting. A problem that occupied him while in Cincinnati was developing a duplex system. This is a system by which two messages could be carried on one wire at the same time. He tried various ideas but had to leave Cincinnati before he arrived at a solution. His temporary job there had come to an end. He was forced to go on his travels again.

Still, Cincinnati was an important milestone in his career. He had gained full mastery of the telegraph. The challenge (after learning Morse code and the special signals) was to send and receive messages quickly. Edison's experience made him as fast as any telegrapher in Cincinnati. He left Cincinnati a "first-class man," to use the terminology of the telegrapher's trade.

Edison went on to Nashville and Memphis. He found Memphis to be a wide-open city. Riverboats going up the Mississippi from New Orleans brought cotton, rice, and timber. They also brought a crowd of colorful, often dangerous, characters—gamblers, gunslingers, and soldiers of fortune. The gambling casinos were open around the clock. There were brawls in the streets. Robberies were common.

Edison avoided the worst of Memphis as much as he could. The job he found there was only part-time. It paid him so little that he was unable to afford the rent at a boardinghouse. He often slept on the floor of the telegrapher's office. Many nights he made his dinner out of old vegetables he picked up for a few pennies at a local market.

In spite of the hardships, Edison again started his experiments with telegraphy. He used the apparatus in the office to test his theories. The office manager found out about this, said he had no right to use the company apparatus, and fired him.

New Orleans was the final stop on Edison's travels through American cities. He did not work as a telegrapher in New Orleans. His plan at this point was to go to South America in search of better opportunity. The plan came to nothing because of the hazards involved. Edison barely had time to see the Mississippi Delta, with its wharves and cotton bales, before he realized that he was stranded in New Orleans.

Edison looked around for another job. He was unable to find anything for which he felt qualified. In any case, his only desire was to be a telegrapher. As the last of his money began to run out, he realized that he could not remain where he was. He also felt a touch of homesickness. Leaving New Orleans, he set out on the long trek north by stage and train to Port Huron.

He arrived in 1867, to a joyful reunion with his family. His mother was especially pleased to see him after his years of wandering through the Midwest and the South. Nancy Edison still had high hopes that her youngest son would amount to something. She listened with great interest, as did his father, to his stories about his work as a tramp telegrapher.

But what was he to do now? His parents had no answer

to that question. Nor did Edison himself until he recalled that Milton Adams, his close friend of the Cincinnati days, had gone to Boston to take a job with Western Union—the biggest telegraph company of the period.

Edison wrote to Adams asking if Western Union had an opening for yet another telegrapher. Adams's reply came by return mail. Yes, there was an opening. The company would feel fortunate to fill it with a telegrapher as expert as Edison. Adams added that he had made arrangements for Edison to be hired. All Edison had to do was get from Port Huron to Boston.

This was easier said than done. It was the dead of winter. Michigan and all the northern states as far as the Atlantic Coast were locked in by ice and snow. The train that Edison took went by way of Canada. It became snowbound and had to stop for the night. It took Edison four days to reach Boston—and there he found the same arctic conditions. He trudged through the city in a howling wind that blew snowflakes all over him.

But it all seemed worthwhile when he was reunited with Milton Adams. His old friend introduced him to the other telegraphers at Western Union. The manager, George Milliken, gave Edison the job after testing his ability at the telegrapher's key.

Edison worked the wire to New York. In doing so, he became a hero to his fellow telegraphers. The Boston office competed with the New York office to see which one could receive messages and translate them from dots and dashes into plain English more rapidly than the other. New York held the upper hand until Edison's arrival in Boston.

Edison got into a contest with New York's fastest sender. The dots and dashes flew between New York and Boston, where Edison wrote out the messages as quickly as he could. Edison never fell behind. He won the contest so easily that, as a joke, he sent his New York rival this message: "Say, young man, change off and send with your other foot!"

Everyone in the Boston office laughed. They slapped him on the back and complimented him on his telegraphic skill. The Bostonians were glad that their new "first-class man" had shown the New Yorkers a thing or two.

Edison stayed in Boston for about a year. He lived in a boardinghouse where Adams also stayed. They resumed their habit of going to operas and concerts together.

Edison also began experimenting in a more professional manner than ever before. He began with theory, buying a set of Michael Faraday's *Experimental Researches in Electricity*. He read straight through. Although not a trained physicist, Edison was able to follow the steps that Faraday had taken in his experiments with electromagnetism, in particular the discovery that an electricity conductor (a metal wire, for instance) moving through a magnetic field produces an electric current. This discovery led to Faraday's invention of the generator in 1831.

The principle of the generator is that if an electricity conductor moves across a magnetic field, an electric current flows into the conductor. For example, if an iron bar (a conductor) is rotated between the ends of a horseshoe-shaped electromagnet, a current enters the bar. The scientific explanation is that mechanical energy is converted into electrical energy. This electrical energy can be used in all kinds of electrical machines.

Faraday's work on electromagnetism influenced Edison's work on electricity. This led in time to Edison's invention of his electric light bulb. However, in 1868, that invention lay more than a decade in the future. Edison could not know that he would later invent a new system of lighting. He was not aware that he was laying the ground for this achievement while he studied Faraday's work for hours on end during his spare time in Boston.

At the same time, Edison was involved in practical experiments. He knew that his experiments might lead to inventions that could be patented. A patent is a government document giving the inventor rights to the invention for a limited time. A patent gives the inventor the right to prevent others from making, using, or selling the invention. In this way the inventor might profit from an invention.

Edison made his first patented invention—a vote recorder—in 1868. Counting and recording votes was a long and boring process in large assemblies or meetings where all the members voted. Edison saw a way to speed up the process.

He strung two wires from each desk to a pad on the dais. The pad held two recorders, one for "yes" votes and one for "no" votes. A member, after deciding which way to vote, pressed one of the keys on his desk. An electrical charge would run along the wire and depress a marker on the pad. The marker would register the vote.

Edison thought he knew one assembly that would welcome his invention—the Congress of the United States. Hoping to gain success, he packaged the instrument and boarded a train to Washington, D.C. Arriving there, he hurried past the national monuments, not pausing at the White House, since there was no chance for him to present his invention to President Andrew Johnson. He went to Capitol Hill, where he was lucky to be received by some members of a committee and allowed to demonstrate his invention.

The committee turned down his suggestion that his vote recorder would benefit both the Senate and the House of Representatives because the registering of votes would be greatly speeded up. Edison asked why they would not accept his vote recorder. One of them explained that the members of Congress did not want to cut down on the time required. They preferred the long process they went through. It allowed them to change their minds while they waited, to hold last-minute consultations, and to ask for a postponement before the voting ended.

"I made up my mind right then," Edison declared, "that I would work on no more inventions that were not practical and did not appeal to a public that would buy them."

His next invention showed what he meant. It was a new form of stock ticker. It appealed to brokers because it brought them Wall Street quotations more quickly. Before the stock ticker, "runners" had to get the figures at the telegraph office and carry them to the brokers. Then wires were introduced in New York City that carried electrical charges from the gold exchange to the brokers' offices. These electrical charges gave the figures quoted for the businesses represented at the stock exchange.

Edison improved this stock ticker by simplifying it. He obtained better results by putting less wire into the machine. Using an alternating current created by two electromagnets, he was able to control two mechanisms at the receiving end—a wheel that turned according to the numbers that arrived over the wire, and a hammer that stamped the numbers on a tape (called a "ticker" tape because of the sound it made as the tape revolved through the stock ticker and fell to the floor).

This was a practical invention. Edison advertised for

clients willing to pay for his services, and about forty brokers and private investors answered his ad.

Nevertheless, he did not make much money. He was still in debt from his previous ventures, and Boston did not offer him enough scope for his ambition. He wanted to become a prominent figure in the world of electricity and telegraphy, and the only place he could do this was New York—the center of American finance and business. Brokers and investors were on Wall Street, buying and selling stocks and bonds, making and losing fortunes. Corporations had their headquarters nearby. Notorious "robber barons" like Cornelius Vanderbilt and Jay Gould were in control of shipping lines and railroads.

Edison therefore decided to try his luck in New York. During the spring of 1869 he caught a boat from Boston to New York. Edison came ashore in Manhattan. He was taking a chance, with little money and no friends to greet him. But he still had all his confidence. He believed his background would enable him to become a success: "Everything I possessed, and everything I had earned since twelve years of age, had been invested in acquiring experience and knowledge."

The first thing he needed in New York was breakfast, but he did not want to spend one of his few coins. Walking through the dock area wondering what to do, he spotted a sign above a store that sold tea. He could see a man inside tasting to see which blends were best.

Edison had an idea. Entering the store, he asked the teataster if he could judge a cup himself. The man agreed, no doubt believing it would be helpful to have the verdict of a member of the public. And so Edison made a breakfast of a cup of tea.

Edison began making the rounds of companies that used telegraphers. One of these was the Gold Indicator Company, which manufactured stock tickers—a mechanism with which Edison was familiar. He hoped to persuade the manager to give him a place on the staff.

One day, while Edison was there, a crisis occurred. The central machine came to a halt. Nobody could get it started again—until Edison came to the rescue. Examining the interior mechanism, he saw that a spring had snapped and fallen down between two wheels that revolved against one another, bringing them to a standstill. Removing the broken spring, he inserted a new one and started the wheels moving again. Everyone present breathed a sigh of relief.

The manager was impressed with Edison's skill. He gave Edison a job at three hundred dollars a month, a large salary in those days. The episode was typical of how Edison made good use of the opportunities that came his way. This job turned his career around, giving him a steady income and allowing him to move ahead with his experiments.

Edison's success at the Gold Indicator Company made him decide to go into business for himself. He joined forces with Franklin Pope, another employee of the firm, and James N. Ashley. On October 2, 1869, they advertised the formation of a new business—Pope, Edison and Company, Electrical Engineers and General Telegraphic Agency.

Pope, Edison and Company had among its customers the Gold and Stock Company. Edison had sold to that company a number of his inventions in the field of telegraphic communications. His universal printer was a new kind of stock ticker. It was such an improvement over the old one that the president of the Gold and Stock Company, Marshall Lefferts, was determined not to let it fall into the hands of a competitor.

Lefferts invited Edison to come to his office for a discussion of how much the rights to the universal printer would cost the Gold and Stock Company. Edison already had some figures in mind. As he settled into a chair in Lefferts's office, he hoped for $5,000 but was prepared to accept $3,000.

He was about to say this when the president of the Gold and Stock Company got in the first word and made an offer. "Will you accept $40,000?" asked Lefferts.

"I never came so near fainting in my life," Edison later confessed. He gulped—and said he would accept the $40,000.

With the money, he expanded a shop he already owned in Newark, New Jersey. He gathered tools, chemicals, wires, cogs, wheels, springs, and mechanisms of all kinds needed in his research. Eventually he gathered a staff as well, giving his employees different problems he devised.

Edison returned to the question of the duplex. How could he develop one telegraphic wire carrying two messages simultaneously? He went beyond this idea and invented the quadruplex, which sent four messages on one wire, two in each direction at the same time. Western Union bought the quadruplex from him. With this invention, Western Union was able to cut in half the number of wires required for its telegraphic system.

Edison remained in Newark for about six years. During that period, he took out many patents in the field of telegraphy. He became famous for his ability to develop new gadgets that could be applied in the electrical and communications industries.

He ended his partnership with Pope and Ashley in 1870 because he felt he was doing all the work. He thus achieved an independence enabling him to research what interested him. With his newfound freedom, he decided to collaborate with Christopher Sholes in perfecting the typewriter in 1871.

That year was one of both tragedy and happiness for Edison.

The tragedy came with the death of his mother. Back in Port Huron, Nancy Edison had been suffering from a long illness. Her son wrote to her regularly from Newark, but his work always seemed to interefere whenever he thought of returning to see her. He felt remorse when news of her death reached him in a telegram from his father. He went to Port Huron for the funeral. But the old surroundings without his mother depressed him. He quickly returned to Newark.

Happiness came to him in 1871 in the form of marriage. There was a young woman named Mary Stilwell who worked in Edison's shop in Newark. Visiting the shop area, Edison noticed Mary and was struck by her youthful beauty and appealing personality. Soon he was inventing reasons to return. The rest of the employees realized he was not there to discuss electricity or telegraphy. His presence became an office joke, much to Mary's embarrassment.

Soon she was accompanying him to the theatrical and musical events that attracted him. They became engaged, were married on Christmas Day of 1871, and found a home in Newark.

Three children were born to the Edisons—Marion Estelle, Thomas Alva, Jr., and William Leslie. Their father playfully gave the two oldest children nicknames drawn from telegraphy. Marion was "Dot" and Thomas was "Dash." He enjoyed romping with them when he returned from work.

Years later Thomas Alva recalled during a newspaper interview: "Although the world remembers my father as a

Mary Stilwell Edison, Thomas Edison's first wife, in 1871, the year they were married.

man of indefatigable [untiring] effort and work, perfecting and inventing the wonders of his age, there was also an intensely human side to him. He was not always so engrossed [completely involved] in his work that he could not spend some time with his children. I remember when he was devising games and recreation for us and the children of the neighborhood...."

The three children were born during the 1870s, a notable decade in Edison's career as an inventor.

CHAPTER

Sounds on a Cylinder

While experimenting in his Newark laboratory, Edison made a discovery in pure science. This point is important because he was really an inventor, not a scientist. As an inventor, he took the scientific discoveries of other individuals and applied them in practical ways.

For example, Faraday's work on electromagnetism caused a scientific revolution. In contrast, Edison's application of electromagnetic principles to the telegraph wire was an invention (or rather a series of inventions). As a scientist, Faraday was mainly interested in theory. Edison the inventor was primarily interested in practice. This is one of the differences between a scientist and an inventor.

However, in 1875, while investigating the application of electromagnets to telegraphy, Edison discovered a type of energy between electromagnetism, on the one hand, and heat and light, on the other. He told his colleagues in the laboratory: "This is simply wonderful...a true unknown force."

He gave it the name "etheric force." In 1887 the German scientist Heinrich Hertz, basing his research partly on Edison's discovery, proved the existence of electromagnetic waves. These are vibrations that include light, X rays, and radio waves. This, in turn, led to Guglielmo Marconi's invention of wireless telegraphy, or radio, in the 1890s. Edison admired Marconi, referring to the Italian inventor as "the young man who had the monumental audacity to attempt and to succeed in jumping an electric wave clear across the Atlantic Ocean." Marconi, in turn, admired Edison because of his discovery of the etheric force. Without that discovery, Marconi's wireless would not have been possible.

In 1876 Edison moved to a new research facility at Menlo Park, now a part of Edison, New Jersey. He wanted to get away from Newark. That city was filled with noisy distractions that made it difficult for him to think about future experiments. He needed to concentrate on business problems. He wanted a more peaceful place, and he found it at Menlo Park.

Here Edison established the world's first research complex devoted to the creation and development of new inventions. Menlo Park prospered. It became a model of the cooperative technological effort that Edison had in mind.

It grew into a number of buildings devoted to different purposes. Edison's office and library were housed in a two-story brick building. There he could get away from the bustle of the laboratory, do his reading and thinking, and plan future experiments. The library held many volumes because Edison read widely on what had already been discovered in any field before venturing into it himself. In that way, he avoided duplicating the work of others. Rather, he began with their findings and advanced further than they had gone.

The most important building at Menlo Park was the long, wooden two-story laboratory. Entering this building, visitors saw a large room occupied on the right by a small office for Edison. Beyond his office were cubicles for research on problems such as light, heat, electricity, and magnetism. Along the left wall of this large room were shelves and cabinets for experimental apparatus and other equipment. A hydraulic press for regulating water pressure stood at one end of the room. A galvanometer, an instrument that measures electric currents, stood at the other end.

From this large, ground-floor room, staff and visitors entered the laboratory shop. There tools and equipment for testing metals were kept along with chemicals, batteries, and whatever else might be needed by members of the staff in carrying out experiments. The second floor held tables for experiments. The battery table remains famous because on it Edison put together the first *practical* electrical light bulb.

Edison brought staff members from Newark to Menlo Park. He added others as they were required. Edison thus had an excellent group of people to handle research under his supervision. The main personnel were all gifted experimenters. Each contributed particular abilities to the common enterprise.

Charles Batchelor, Edison's chief assistant, was a genius with machinery. Francis Upton received critical assignments in mathematical physics. John Kruesi came from Switzerland and rose to become foreman of the shop. Francis Jehl, an Austrian, had an important part in developing the electric light bulb. Two brothers, John and Frederick Ott, were machinists and draftsmen.

Edison hired his specialists wherever he found them, gave them instructions, and then allowed them a large measure of freedom. In this way, Edison pioneered organized technical research, the kind that has ever since been indispensable in industrial laboratories. Menlo Park had a "team," and Edison was its "captain."

Edison devoted the year 1876 to a number of inventions. One was the mimeograph machine. Using an electric pen, he made punctures (representing letters) in a piece of waxed paper, which was placed on a drum. A felt roller soaked with ink moved across the waxed paper. It transferred the puncture marks to a sheet below. The waxed paper was the stencil, from which any number of copies could be made.

The year after moving into Menlo Park, Edison made the first of his three greatest inventions, the phonograph (the other two were his electric light bulb and his motion-picture camera).

The phonograph was based on the fact that a vibrating surface, called a diaphragm, can pick up sounds caused by a stylus, or needle, which makes indentations on a blank record. When the needle is returned to its starting point on the record, and moves along the original path, the diaphragm reproduces the original sounds. These sounds may be as diverse as human speech, bird songs, the roar of ocean surf, or orchestral music.

The use of diaphragms in acoustical science was a familiar fact when Edison began his work. Alexander Graham Bell invented the telephone in 1875 when he attached a diaphragm to an iron bar and added an electromagnet to the mechanism. The human voice caused the diaphragm to vibrate as the sounds struck it. An electric current transmitted the sounds along a wire. The sounds were reproduced by the magnetic receiver at the other end of the wire.

Edison improved the telephone by placing carbon in the form of lampblack (soot) inside Bell's mechanism. This increased the sound and made it easier for the listener to recognize the words of the speaker. Then Edison began to experiment with diaphragms in various ways, until one day he heard sounds not merely *transmitted*, but *reproduced*—a discovery from which the phonograph evolved.

For the first phonograph ever built, Edison put a cylinder on a shaft, with a handle for turning the cylinder. He placed a diaphragm at each end of the cylinder. The cylinder was wrapped in tinfoil. Sound waves hitting the diaphragms would cause them to vibrate. A needle moving across the tinfoil would record different sounds by scratching grooves of different depths as it went along.

According to Edison's theory, when the needle was returned to its original position, and moved along its original path as the handle was turned, the original words should be repeated by the diaphragm vibrations. When the machine was ready, Edison called members of his staff to listen to it. They were all doubtful that it would work.

Starting the needle by cranking the cylinder, Edison recited the nursery rhyme "Mary had a little lamb/Its fleece was white as snow." Then he returned the needle to its original position and cranked the cylinder without saying anything. Everybody waited patiently. Suddenly the machine broke the silence by repeating the words "Mary had a little lamb/Its fleece was white as snow."

The audience gave a loud cheer at this, the first time

The first phonograph recorded sound on a cylinder wrapped in tinfoil.
This famous photograph, taken in 1888, shows Edison with his wax
cylinder type of phonograph.

anyone had ever heard a phonograph recording. It was not exactly what we mean by a phonograph because the state of the art keeps progressing far beyond Edison's 1877 invention. The cumbersome machine he used on that first occasion in his laboratory gave way to the simple disk on a turntable, for which an inventor named Emile Berliner was mainly responsible. In recent times, cassettes and CDs (compact disks) have been replacing turntable disks, or records.

Edison recorded different sound vibrations by letting the stylus vary the depth of the grove. This became known as the "hill and dale" method—the needle going "up hill and down dale" as it moved from shallow groves to deep ones, back to shallow, and so on. Today the *width* of the groove captures different vibrations. The needle repeats these vibrations as it moves from wide grooves to narrow ones, back to wide, and so on.

Yet the principle remains the same. In all essentials, the present-day phonograph is the one Edison invented. It is, moreover, the one invention for which he was entirely responsible. He did not, as is often said, invent the electric light bulb, which was already known to other inventors. He invented the *practical* light bulb. In the same way, other inventors were experimenting with motion-picture cameras when Edison came up with a practical camera.

But it had never occurred to another inventor to attempt to record the human voice. The phonograph was Edison's invention—and nobody else's.

"Which do I consider my greatest invention?" he once said in answer to a question. "Well, my reply to that would be that I like the phonograph best. Doubtless this is because I love music. And then, it has brought so much joy into millions of homes all over this country, and, indeed, all over the world."

The fame of the phonograph spread, and the machine proved to be a financial success when Edison put it on the market. At first it seemed to be nothing more than a toy. But its serious possibilities soon became apparent. Singers were particularly attracted to it as a means of recording their voices for listeners who might not have the opportunity to hear them in the opera houses. Enrico Caruso, the great Italian tenor, recognized the effectiveness of the phonograph. He made many recordings. Those that survive are some of the discs most prized by collectors. If it hadn't been for Edison, we would have to guess what Caruso's voice sounded like.

In 1878 Edison went to Washington, D.C., at the request of the National Academy of Sciences. The members of that learned body were eager to hear his phonograph and to test it for themselves. A large crowd of scientists filled the room where the demonstration took place. Charles Batchelor was with Edison. The two demonstrated how the machine would repeat words spoken into it. At the end, the scientists broke into loud applause. They crowded around Edison and Batchelor for a discussion of the physical laws explaining the phenomenon.

Edison met a number of senators and members of the House of Representatives at the home of a Washington, D.C., hostess, Gail Hamilton. Edison chose the nursery rhyme "There was a little girl, who had a little curl/Right in the middle of her forehead." The phonograph repeated the lines. The listeners were amazed by what they heard. Those who had been skeptical were finally convinced of the reality of Edison's talking machine.

President Rutherford B. Hayes, having learned that Edison was in town with his phonograph, invited him to bring his invention to the White House. The president enjoyed some lighter moments with the phonograph. He asked the first lady to listen to the astonishing marvel of a talking machine. Mrs. Hayes was a prim person, known as "Lemonade Lucy" because she never served anything stronger than lemonade at the White House. She was already in bed because Edison arrived late in the evening. But she willingly dressed and came down to join the group around the phonograph. The president and first lady were so taken by the invention that they kept Edison at the White House until the wee hours of the morning.

Back home in Menlo Park, Edison decided to make a trip west with a scientific group covering a solar eclipse. Astronomers knew that the blotting out of the sun would be visible in the Rocky Mountains. They therefore arranged to be at the best places to watch the eclipse at the time.

Edison became involved because of his invention of a highly sensitive tasimeter. The tasimeter is an instrument that measures very small changes in temperature. His tasimeter interested astronomers. They wanted to measure changes in the temperature of the corona, the radiant ring around the sun, before, during, and after the eclipse.

Two Princeton professors, Rufus Brackett and Charles Young, visited Menlo Park and explained their need for a tasimeter. Edison built a special instrument for them. They took it to Colorado, where they had selected their site for watching the eclipse.

New York University was sending a scientific group to Wyoming. One member, Professor Henry Draper, Edison's friend, appealed to the inventor for another tasimeter.

Edison provided it and agreed to go along on the expedition. He wanted to watch his invention in action, and to have a vacation after a long period of keeping his nose to the grindstone in his laboratory.

Edison and his friends traveled to Wyoming by train. Only nine years had passed since the driving of a golden spike that joined the rails from the East and West at Promontory, Utah, creating the transcontinental railroad. But even in this brief time, side routes called spurs had been laid from the major lines to out-of-the-way places. One such place was Rawlins, Wyoming, the destination of the scientists from New York University.

Edison and his friends rode across the continent to the High Plains near the Rocky Mountains. This was the Wild West. Wyoming was not a state, only a territory (statehood would come in 1890). In 1876 the defeat and killing of General George Armstrong Custer and his troops by the Sioux Indians under Sitting Bull had taken place north of the Wyoming border on the Little Bighorn in Montana. Edison arrived in Wyoming only two years after Custer's Last Stand.

Rawlins, west of Laramie and Cheyenne, was a rough western town. Cowboys brought herds of cattle there to sell. They celebrated payday with cards, dice, hard liquor, and frequently with gunfire in the streets.

It is not surprising that Edison ran into a gunslinger who might have stepped out of a western movie. Known as Texas Jack, this character sported two revolvers at his belt and claimed to be the fastest gun in Wyoming. He pushed his way into Edison's hotel room, looking as if he wanted a showdown with its occupant. However, Texas Jack said he merely wanted to shake the hand of the inventor of the phonograph. Edison's companions had mentioned the marvelous instrument that "talked" like a human being. Gossip about it had spread through this rip-roaring town of the Wyoming Territory. Even its most notorious gunslinger wanted to pay his respects to the inventor. Before leaving, Texas Jack gave Edison a display of precision shooting through the hotel window.

Many other stories came out of Edison's trip to Wyoming. On one occasion, Edison rode the cowcatcher (the frame on the front of the train) as the locomotive barreled along at high speed. It struck what appeared to be a bear cub. The animal flipped through the air toward Edison, who ducked just in time to escape being knocked off his perch and probably killed by falling from the moving train to the ground.

Another time Edison stalked a jack rabbit, rifle in hand, hit it with several shots, failed to make it move, and discovered it was stuffed. One of his friends had played a practical joke on him.

As for the solar eclipse, the astronomers gathered a lot of information. But Edison's tasimeter did them little good. It was too sensitive for their purpose. It registered tiny degrees of heat around the telescope, mingling this with the heat of the sun's corona. So the experiment was spoiled.

After the eclipse, Edison traveled west all the way to San Francisco. At Virginia City, Nevada, the mining of gold and silver was creating fortunes overnight. Edison went down into a mine and saw how the miners drilled into the rock in search of the precious metals. The idea occurred to him that gold and silver, which are good conductors of electricity, might be found by applying an electrical current to the rock faces. That would make the backbreaking work unnecessary.

He never figured out how this might be accomplished, nor did anyone else. The old, hard, dirty, dusty, mining methods continued.

Edison returned home by train, again crossing the Great Divide of North America. He traveled across high mountains and broad plains. Reaching the Missouri River, he crossed over and continued on east. He must have recalled the prairie schooners he had seen as a boy, headed west toward the California gold fields. Now Edison was ending a transcontinental journey in the comfort of a railroad car, covering, in a few hours, vast distances that had once taken weeks to journey across.

Back home, Edison resumed experimenting in his laboratory at Menlo Park. Although electricity was now the subject he preferred, he set it aside temporarily when a New Jersey farmer asked him if he could devise a spray to kill the potato bugs that infested the planted fields. Edison experimented with chemicals in various combinations. He poured carefully measured proportions from beakers into bowls and drained off samples into test tubes.

Trying the samples on potato bugs kept in jars on his workbench, he found that one compound, bisulphide of carbon, did the trick better than any other. When he took the bugs from the jars and sprayed them, none survived.

Edison carried his bisulphide of carbon to the farm, explained its effect to the farmer, and proceeded to spray the infested areas. It killed all the bugs he sprayed. And that seemed to solve the problem. But the next day the farmer arrived with news that Edison's spray had killed the plants along with the bugs.

Edison knew what had caused his failure: "I did not control the experiment properly." He realized he should have tried the spray on the plants as well as the bugs while experimenting at his workbench. He never again allowed himself to forget that conditions inside the laboratory might not be the same as those outside. *He learned from his mistake.*

Because of his growing interest in electric lighting, Edison was pleased when Grosvenor Porter Lowrey, a Wall Street lawyer, came to him with a proposal. Lowrey asked if Edison would be interested in setting up a company to support further research. Edison replied that he would be very interested. His reputation was so great that Lowrey was able to find backers, including, J.P. Morgan, America's leading financier, who were willing to put up money to support the project. Lowrey's proposal lead to the creation of the Edison Electric Light Company in 1878. This organization became one of the great American corporations. It was the most important of the companies that joined forces to create General Electric Company, which remains today a world leader in the development of electrical power for industrial progress.

Edison was now one of the most famous men in America. Some people thought he could invent anything. His next great invention seemed to prove them right. It was his electric light bulb.

Lighting the World

Edison had been thinking off and on about the problems of lighting by means of electricity. As usual, he had gathered a shelf of books on the subject. He knew from his reading that inventors in several countries were searching for a practical method of controlling incandescence. Incandescence is the light emitted, or sent out, by a substance when heated to a high enough degree, a red-hot iron bar, for instance.

It was known that a generator sending a current through a wire into a vacuum would cause a filament (the wire) to become hot enought to glow. Much of Edison's success with electric lighting came from his improvement of the generator. His famous "Long-Waisted Mary Ann" was a larger, more energy-efficient generator than any other. It had two cores, each one four feet tall, creating electrical currents. Other generators lost about 50 percent of their energy. Edison's new design cut that to 30 percent. The difference allowed him to build powerhouses that produced more powerful electrical charges than any other then in operation.

Shortly after inventing the "Long-Waisted Mary Ann," in 1879, Edison donated a generator to the *Jeannette*, a ship assigned to Arctic exploration. The Edison generator ran a system of arc lighting in which an electric current flowing between two carbon rods produced light.

Arc lighting was effective for large-scale operations, such as illumination aboard the *Jeannette*. But it produced too powerful a glare and used too much voltage for private use. That was the reason for the international search for practical incandescent lighting. Experiments were based on the fact that a generator sending a current through a wire into a vacuum would cause a filament to become hot enough to glow. The difficulty was that every tested filament burned out shortly after emitting light. The unsolved problem was to find a filament that would last long enough to be part of a practical electric light bulb.

Edison set out to solve this problem. His first theory was that a platinum filament would have the necessary endurance. He was so sure of himself that he announced it as a fact. This announcement caused the price of gas stocks to tumble. People believed he would now replace gas lighting with electricity.

Edison's announcement that he had a practical filament was premature. True enough, he was correct in thinking platinum would glow and produce light. But his experiments at Menlo Park revealed that platinum reached its melting point too soon.

Edison kept trying many other substances without

A model of Edison's first electric lamp.

success. He then turned to carbon. He took a cotton thread and covered it with powdered carbon. Next he heated it to a high degree. The carbon stuck to the thread. The thread became his filament. Sending a current into this filament, he found that it would stay lighted for forty hours before burning out. Unlike other inventors, who failed with short, thick filaments, Edison succeeded with a long, thin filament.

The vacuum he needed was inside a glass bulb from which the air had been pumped. A wire running from his generator to the filament inside the bulb provided the current.

Edison made this invention in 1879. He patented it in 1880. Edison described it as "an electric lamp for giving light by incandescence, consisting of a filament of carbon of high resistance, made as described, and secured to metallic wires, as set forth."

The United States Patent Office in Washington, D.C., found that Edison had no competition in the field of practical incandescent electric lighting. It gave him his patent. In London there was some opposition to Edison by backers of Joseph Swan, who had been working on his own version of an electric light bulb. The two inventors finally ended the dispute by forming the Edison & Swan United Electric Light Company in 1883. It controlled electric lighting in Great Britain for many years.

After Edison's invention of his electric light bulb came the development of a comprehensive system of power, wiring, and bulbs. Wanting to make a dramatic public exhibition, Edison announced that he would light up Menlo Park with electricity on New Year's Eve in 1879. He had a generator set up, wires strung, and lighting installed inside the buildings and outside.

When the time came for the display, an enormous crowd was on hand. People came in wagons and on horse-back. They came by railroad from New York and Phila-delphia. They walked from nearby towns and farms. They gathered at Menlo Park, waiting in high anticipation for the moment when the renowned inventor would show his latest invention.

Edison courteously let his visitors tramp through his laboratory. He explained his electric lighting as simply as he could. Reporters from the newspapers questioned him about the future of his invention. He predicted that it would revolutionize lighting around the world.

When the great moment came, Edison turned on the lights. The darkness was gone. Glittering light bulbs revealed Menlo Park as it had never been seen before. The onlookers gasped in delight, and then broke into wild cheering. None of them—indeed nobody anywhere in the world—had ever seen anything like this first demonstration of incandescent electric lights on a large scale. Many visitors stayed all night. All went home to talk of the marvels they had seen at Menlo Park.

A year later Edison put on another and much larger display at Menlo Park. This time he had thousands of light bulbs strung outside the buildings and hundreds of lamps inside. The effect was even greater than the year before.

In 1880 Edison put incandescent electric lighting aboard the vessel *Columbia*, the first time this system was ever used as a commercial venture.

That same year Edison also adapted electricity to land transportation. He built a small-scale electric train on the grounds at Menlo Park. The locomotive was much smaller than the giant steam locomotives already on the rails across

America. However, Edison intended to go into professional railroading if he could find buyers for his invention. It would serve as a model for large-scale machines.

His locomotive was a small open vehicle. The engineer sat just behind one of the wheels, his feet nearly touching it. A battery close to his knee provided the power to draw a car holding more than twenty passengers.

The train proved to be a success on its test run. In later runs, Edison himself often took over the controls. On one occasion he hit a curve at such high speed that he caused the locomotive to jump the tracks. Everyone aboard was thrown to the ground, fortunately without anyone suffering serious injury. He termed the accident "beautiful," meaning that it occurred because the train worked so well.

After the accident, Edison closed in the engineer's cab and covered over the motor up ahead, making his invention look more like an ordinary train. This model was one that many trainmen and businessmen came to inspect. So did representatives of foreign governments who hoped their transportation problems might be solved by Edison's electric train.

One such foreign delegation came from a South American nation. After watching a demonstration of the train on level ground, they noted that their country had many steep mountainsides. Would the electric locomotive generate enough power to climb up to the passes leading to the other side of the mountains?

Edison prepared a special test. He had tracks laid up a steep hill. He then showed his South American visitors that his machine could easily make the grade to the top of the hill. They expressed satisfaction with what they had seen. They assured Edison that they would recommend his train

Edison's electric railway at Menlo Park, New Jersey, in 1880.

to their government and get back to him. Then they left for home.

The result? Edison told the joke on himself like this: "I have never seen them since. As usual, I paid for the experiment."

Although Edison's train served as a model for electrical railroading later on, he did not participate in this development. He did not get enough backers to put up money for the enterprise. As he had vowed earlier when his vote recorder was rejected in Washington, he would not continue with any invention for which there was no market.

Among the many visitors who came to see Edison at Menlo Park was Sarah Bernhardt—the "Divine Sarah"—the world-famous actress of the French stage. In 1880 Sarah Bernhardt made a tour of America. While she was in New York, she agreed to make a side trip to Menlo Park to see Edison. Her public relations release stated that "the most famous man in America should have the pleasure of meeting the most famous woman in France."

It was arranged that Bernhardt would go directly from the New York theater after her final performance in *Camille*. Bernhardt always received an enthusiastic welcome from American audiences, and this last occasion in New York was no exception. She said, in recalling the experience, that she took twenty-nine curtain calls at the repeated demands of her admirers. She added that when she made her exit from the theater she was mobbed by autograph seekers.

Bernhardt started out for Menlo Park late in the evening, arriving there after midnight. From the train, she drove by carriage through the darkness, which was suddenly broken by what looked like a fairyland of lights. Edison had turned them on for her benefit.

When the "Divine Sarah" descended from the carriage, Edison bowed over her hand and invited her to see everything at Menlo Park that interested her. They talked animatedly as they walked around the laboratory. Her later comment was that "in half-an-hour we were the best friends in the world."

Amazed by the turning on and off of electric lights, she asked: "Will we ever have electricity in the theater?" Yes, Edison replied. He went on to explain that any type of building could be illuminated with electric lights.

She also spoke over the telephone to one of Edison's assistants. But the invention that really captivated her was the phonograph. Here was a machine that could record her voice—the voice that enchanted so many theater audiences. She spoke some eloquent lines from Racine, the greatest of French dramatists. She was enraptured when the machine repeated her words.

Edison then sang "Yankee Doodle"—off-key, for he was no Caruso—and the machine's repetition made her giggle. She might have stayed at Menlo Park all night except that she had to leave to catch a train to Boston. She departed comparing Edison to Napoleon.

Sarah Bernhardt was an artist as well as an actress. She sent some paintings from her workshop in Paris, offering them to Edison as "The Giver of Light."

During the 1880s, Edison became involved with the world of adventure when he was trying to find a better substance for the filaments in his light bulbs. He wanted to extend the time a filament would stay lighted. His carbonized thread had lasted for forty hours. A special type of cardboard set a record of more than one hundred hours. If he could push the duration even higher, he would make it possible for electric lighting to stay on for longer periods without a breakdown.

One day, in 1880, Edison noticed a fan with a bamboo rim on a table in his home. Struck by a sudden inspiration, as he often was, he clipped off the bamboo, took it to his laboratory, carbonized it, and tested it as a filament. It lasted longer than anything he had yet tried. He therefore began making bamboo filaments for his light bulbs.

But there were many varieties of bamboo. Was the bamboo from the fan the best for his purposes? He could not know without testing the others in his laboratory. American varieties were easily obtainable. Those in Asia and South America had to be located and brought home. As a result, Edison commissioned adventurous individuals to go into the jungles on special bamboo-hunting expeditions.

One such individual was Frank McGowan, who traveled in the dense rain forests of South America in the years 1887 and 1888. McGowan had to endure heat, rain, swamps, insects, reptiles, and fever that forced him to stay in his tent for days at a time before he finished his trek. He sent back a consignment of bamboo from Colombia.

Another of Edison's adventurers, James Ricalton, was an educator from Maplewood, New Jersey. In 1888 Ricalton took time off from his rather humdrum educational duties to travel around the world. Edison persuaded Ricalton to look for bamboo in India, Burma, China, and Japan. Ricalton returned with varieties of bamboo native to those countries.

Edison used bamboo for filaments. This remained standard until it became obsolete by the discovery of cellulose, a substance found in plant cells. Later, the metal tungsten was found to be superior to every other substance. This remains the material used in electric light bulbs today.

In 1882 Edison began to make a profitable success of his incandescent lighting system. He built a power plant in London and lighted the area around Holborn Viaduct. Moving into New York City, he strung more than eight hundred light bulbs around the Pearl Street station. He then turned on his generators and provided illumination for about fifty businesses.

Meeting newspaper reporters afterward, Edison told them: "I have accomplished what I promised." He might have added that he had opened the way to lighting the world with electricity. The gaslight era was coming to an end.

In 1881 Edison had founded another company to exploit his inventions. This was the Edison Machine Works in New York City, where it was situated for five years. Then a strike and other difficulties forced him to look elsewhere. He sent his agents up the Hudson River in search of a site. They reported that Schenectady, on the Mohawk River near Albany, would be the best choice.

Accepting their advice, Edison purchased two buildings in Schenectady from a locomotive company. These buildings were the center from which his own company would expand. Private citizens and local businesses knew about Edison's reputation as both an inventor and a businessman and were eager to have his factory in their city.

Edison moved the Edison Machine Works to Schenectady. He constructed more buildings as they were needed. There he ran a thriving business turning out generators for his electrical generating stations.

In 1889 he joined together this and several other companies with the Edison General Electric Company. Three years later, in one of the great mergers in the history of American industry, the Edison General Electric Company joined forces with the Thomson-Houston Company in Schenectady. Thomson-Houston brought to the partnership a market it had developed for products derived from its own research into lighting and electricity. The Edison General Electric Company contributed Edison's patents for the electric light, his generator, and his business organization.

The partners called their new enterprise the General Electric Company. A success from its beginnings, it grew into the titan of the industry. Many important discoveries have been made in General Electric laboratories by great names in electrical engineering. The greatest name in company history, after Edison, is Charles Proteus Steinmetz, a German electrical engineer who had come to the United States in 1889. Steinmetz worked as a consulting engineer at General Electric, beginning in 1893. Steinmetz was responsible for the law of hysteresis. This law concerns the loss of electrical power caused by a changing magnetizing force. At General Electric, Steinmetz and Edison knew each other. They developed the mutual admiration of two geniuses. Steinmetz said of Edison: "He has done more than any other man to promote the art and science of electrical engineering."

Edison said that Steinmetz "never mentioned mathematics when he talked to me." Edison appreciated this because he was never good at mathematics. It was not a failing to be embarrassed about—even the great chemist and physicist Michael Faraday was no mathematician. Edison had assistants who could do the calculations needed in laboratory experiments and industrial engineering. He himself stuck to the area in which he excelled—practical inventions.

The Wizard of Menlo Park

wo of Edison's greatest inventions—the phonograph and the electric light bulb—came out of his laboratory at Menlo Park. But many other achievements added to the glory of those "golden years."

Edison's work on the telegraph and the telephone figured enormously in making practical, profitable business enterprises of the inventions of Morse (telegraph) and Bell (telephone). He kept going back over his own inventions as new ideas for the phonograph and the electric light bulb continued to occur to him. He was constantly involved with new inventions, such as his generators and his electric train.

In 1880 Edison made another discovery in pure science. He noticed that if a metal plate is inserted into an electric light bulb between the ends of the filament, the plate becomes a valve by which the current can be controlled. The scientific explanation is that small particles called electrons flow from the filament to the plate. By changing the position of the plate, the electrons can be either stopped or allowed through.

This discovery is known in science as the "Edison Effect." It is the basis for the whole field of electronics, which, however, Edison himself did not pursue.

His inventions were so revolutionary, and his patents so numerous, that in the popular imagination it seemed that he was coming up with a new mysterious gadget every day. He was known far and wide as "the Wizard of Menlo Park."

Edison's private life changed in 1884. His first wife died, leaving him with three children. He could not take care of them properly, since he had to be at the laboratory most of the time. Fate took care of this problem in 1885 when he met Mina Miller of Akron, Ohio.

Mina came from a wealthy, cultured family. Her father, Lewis Miller, was an inventor who made a fortune by improving agricultural machinery. He was also an educator who took part in the Chautauqua movement, which provided free lectures for the public. His daughter enjoyed advantages at an early age, including a tour of Europe.

Edison and Mina Miller seem to have taken to each other at their first meeting in the home of mutual friends. They got along despite the disparity in their ages—he was thirty-eight, and she was twenty. The effect she had on him can still be read in his diary: "Saw a lady who looked like Mina. Got thinking about Mina and came near being run over by a street car. If Mina interferes much more will have to take out an accident policy."

They were often separated because Mina was in either Akron, Ohio, or Chautauqua, in western New York State. At last Edison went to Chautauqua determined to ask her to marry him. In those days of the Victorian age, a young lady was expected to have a chaperon when receiving a gentleman caller. Besides this, Edison's deafness prevented their conversing in whispers. What could they do about it?

Always inventive, Edison gave Mina a crash course in Morse code. By tapping their fingers, they were able to exchange brief messages. At the critical moment, Edison tapped his proposal on Mina's palm. Mina responded without difficulty, as all she had to say in Morse code was "yes."

Edison wrote a formal request to Lewis Miller, who agreed to the marriage. Miller believed Edison would make a good husband for his daughter. Perhaps he also enjoyed the thought of having someone in the family who was a better inventor than himself.

The wedding took place in Akron on February 24, 1886. The newlyweds left for a honeymoon in Fort Myers, Florida, where Edison was building a house on the Caloosahatchee River. This house became their winter home.

Mina Edison now took charge of her husband's three children. It was not easy for her because they, especially daughter Marion, resented her. But Mina had tact and good sense. In time they came to accept her.

Three children were born of Edison's second marriage, Madeleine (1888), Charles (1890), and Theodore (1898). Interestingly, the pattern for his two sets of children was the same—a daughter followed by two sons.

Of the six, Charles was the most successful. Charles worked closely with his father and held a large measure of control over Edison enterprises before Edison's death. Later, Charles Edison went into the Washington bureaucracy and rose to become secretary of the navy. Entering politics successfully, he served as governor of New Jersey from 1941

*Thomas Edison, his wife Mina, and their children, Madeleine,
Charles, and Theodore. One of the two women in the back row may be
Edison's daughter from his first marriage.*

to 1944. Only Madeleine had children. Since they bore the name of their father, John Sloane, the Edison name was destined to die out with the passing of Edison's last surviving child, Theodore Edison.

At the time of their marriage, Edison asked his second wife whether she wanted a town house in New York City or a house in the countryside. Mina chose the latter. They found what they wanted in Glenmont, a mansion with eleven acres in Llewellyn Park, at West Orange, New Jersey.

The mansion came on the market because its previous owner, a department store executive, was caught in an embezzlement scheme and escaped abroad. He had the house sold to pay his creditors. It was almost new, having been built by architect H. Hudson Holly during the period from 1880 to 1881.

Glenmont was a striking structure with numerous tall chimneys and triangular gables slanting upward. One part of the roof was a flat open space surrounded by a railing from which an observer could get a long view over the Orange Valley. A sun room at one corner of the house admitted enough sunlight through enormous windows for the maintenance of potted plants inside. The veranda was of raised stones.

Inside there were twenty-three rooms. A wide staircase led from the first story to the second. Some rooms on the ground floor had wood paneling. Large chandeliers hung from the ceilings. There were animal-skin rugs on the floors. Sunlight filtered through stained-glass windows. The Edisons lived in a beautiful home filled with magnificent furniture, sculpture, and pictures.

Thomas Alva and Mina Edison set aside one room on the second floor for their combined office and study. Often,

Edison working in his West Orange, New Jersey, chemistry laboratory.

Edison would sit in an easy chair reading while his wife sat at the desk working on family accounts. They kept a staff of more than a dozen servants to take care of their mansion.

The Edisons lived at Glenmont for forty-five years. The couple complemented one another, each contributing something unique to their marriage, which was a happy one. While Edison was preoccupied with his work at the laboratory, Mina presided over their home. She gave the servants their assignments, paid the bills, took care of such things as heating and repairs, and worked in the garden. She also saw to the education of the children, including practice on the piano that occupied one room at Glenmont.

In 1887 Edison established his great laboratory complex at West Orange. It became a perfect example of what he meant by industrial research. He now had a larger plant than Menlo Park, and a bigger staff to go with it. He pictured West Orange as a place where many experimenters pooled their efforts to make inventions that would be profitable when placed on the market.

He therefore planned West Orange very carefully to meet his basic requirements. When the buildings were erected, he moved in apparatus for all kinds of experiments and inventions. The years that followed were among his most creative.

Edison's office in the main building held many shelves of books. His desk—its drawers and pigeonholes filled with documents—faced away from a long table around which he and his assistants gathered to thrash out ideas. They planned new projects, and decided whether experiments underway should continue or be canceled as failures. To one side of his desk, a statue carved in Italy and bought by Edison at the Paris Universal Exposition in 1889 held aloft an electric light bulb. The statue represented the "Genius of Electricity."

Smaller rooms in the main building were devoted to specialized subjects, such as machinery and photography. Outside there were storage vaults, a powerhouse, and laboratories where experiments in physics, chemistry, and metallurgy were carried out.

The buildings in West Orange are maintained as they were in Edison's time. The chemistry laboratory is especially interesting because chemistry was Edison's favorite science. From the doorway, tables line both sides of the laboratory. Racks on the tables and shelves underneath hold line after line of bottles that once were filled with the chemicals Edison used in his experiments. The basins in which he mixed his chemicals are still in evidence. His protective gown and mask hang on a peg beneath an electric fan as if he had just placed them there.

One can almost feel the presence of Edison as he bustled around his chemical laboratory, taking down bottles and mixing their contents, even the most dangerous, such as poisons and corrosives. We can imagine him watching intently as they hissed, bubbled, and occasionally exploded.

The typical inventor is often pictured as a lonely individual. The typical inventor is thought to be difficult to get along with, struggling against poverty, ignored by the public, living and dying in obscurity. Edison was the reverse of this. Far from working in isolation, Edison thrived in a beehive of organized productivity. He was surrounded by dozens of assistants who were his staunchest admirers. They put up with his occasional bad temper because they knew he was a genius. They felt privileged to work with him. And instead of being ignored by the public, he achieved worldwide fame.

Though Edison made millions, he was sometimes short of funds because his projects were very expensive. He wanted money so that he could continue his work: "I always invent to obtain money to go on inventing." A sign in the West Orange laboratory read: "Save the juice, save the juice/ Switch off the light when not in use."

West Orange, with its vast laboratory research concentrated on well-defined problems on a broad scale, was something new in the world. It became the forerunner of many similar institutions to come. Today, it is possible to visit this industrial research laboratory, which has been called one of Edison's greatest inventions. Since 1956 the West Orange plant has been maintained as the Edison National Historic Site by the National Park Service of the U.S. Department of the Interior.

But Edison was still called "the Wizard of Menlo Park." The nickname remained popular. There would have been no point in trying to replace it with "the Wizard of West Orange."

With Glenmont so close to his West Orange laboratory, Edison was able to get home quickly when he quit work. His schedule varied. While preoccupied with an experiment, he would frequently take catnaps in the laboratory in order to continue the experiment immediately upon awakening. At other times he might stick to a problem for twenty hours on end. Returning home tired and sleepy, he often fell into bed and slept for twenty hours.

His wife gave him her full support. She provided a tranquil home atmosphere where he could relax in peace and quiet. This made up for the labor, noise, and bustle at the laboratory. Mina Edison saw to it that he was shielded from any interruptions when he was relaxing.

Thomas and Mina Edison, in his West Orange, New Jersey, research center in 1906.

A simple routine at home satisfied Edison because he had no hobbies. He did not play cards, billiards, tennis, or golf. He did not go swimming. He did not go to ball games or follow sports as a spectator. A walk in the garden or a ride in the car was all he needed as a diversion.

Of course, the family was concerned about Edison's deafness. As time passed, it became increasingly difficult for him to make out what other people were saying. He would have gone out in public much less frequently if his wife had not been there to help him with conversations. He was so accustomed to her voice that he could comprehend what she was saying when other people's voices failed to register with him. So, when she saw he was in trouble, she would repeat the words in a manner he could understand. They became so adept at communicating in this way that some persons who talked to Edison in the company of his wife scarcely realized she was interpreting for him.

Edison continued to be a great reader. Toward the end of his life, Mina Edison wrote: "At home he always sits under the brilliant lamp reading as though he would devour all the books that were ever printed. He reads two or three lines at a time. Most of us read words—he reads whole sentences—more than whole sentences if they happen to be short ones. I have never seen anyone concentrate as he does."

Shakespeare remained one of his favorite authors. He especially admired *Othello* for its presentation of highly personalized drama. Perhaps what held Edison's attention was the fact that Othello's problems are all in his mind. The construction of the play—Shakespeare's ability to make ideas have profound practical consequences—might have reminded Edison of laboratory experiments. Shakespeare, he argued, "would have made a great inventor."

Edison also read the works of Victor Hugo, whose *Les Misérables* portrayed life, especially that of the lower classes in France, in realistic terms. But Edison also had his lighter moments in his reading. He liked Alexandre Dumas's swashbuckling stories of *The Three Musketeers* and *The Count of Monte Cristo*. He read detective stories and even the *Police Gazette*. Sometimes he read to be moved by great literature. At other times, he wanted to be amused. And yet again, he was searching for information about the world in which he lived.

When he was with his friends, and serious matters had been taken care of, Edison would ask for the latest stories that were going around. He responded to funny stories with gales of laughter. He was a good mimic and often imitated other people. And he enjoyed practical jokes. One was to put strange messages on a hidden phonograph, turn on the machine secretly, and watch the reaction. He laughed heartily when one guest fled from the room as the hidden phonograph intoned "Prepare to die!"

Edison continued to be physically active into his later years. On his seventy-third birthday, he challenged his guests to see who could kick the highest. Some were much younger than Edison, but they lost the contest.

The fact that he remained physically sound explains why he could push himself so hard in the laboratory. His going without sleep when he had a project in hand did not slow him down. He shrugged off accidents in the laboratory, as he did when a mixture of chloride of sulphur exploded into his eyes. Although he could not see properly for sometime afterward, his sight returned to normal.

Nor did intense concentration harm him. His mind remained clear throughout his life. He was as capable of following a logical chain of ideas at seventy as he had been at thirty.

With his laboratory staff, Edison was all work, except for an annual outing. Then everybody took the day off. They went to a field for a picnic, relaxation in the shade of the trees, strolls through the woods, and games like horseshoe pitching and baseball.

Edison never missed the annual outings if he could be there. He enjoyed throwing out the first ball for the baseball game. Then he joined in the applause and the cheering as his hired hands swung bats, chased flies, and ran the bases.

At one annual outing, Edison saluted the "old-timers" who had been with him for many years. Mrs. Edison draped a sash around the shoulders of the "old-timer" who had been on the staff the longest—William H. Meadowcroft, Edison's personal secretary. Meadowcroft's books about the inventor later became a basic source of information regarding his life.

In 1889 the Edisons took one of their rare vacations. They went to Europe. As they came ashore at Le Havre, a delegation of French dignitaries met them. They saluted Edison as the genius behind the phonograph and the electric light. His arrival in Paris led to a triumphal tour of the French capital. He and Mrs. Edison were received at the Elysée Palace by the president of the French Republic, Sadi Carnot. The president decorated Edison with the Legion of Honor. They went to the Paris Exposition, where Edison's inventions were on display.

Crowds gathered at their hotel, cheering every time Edison came to the window and raised his hand in acknowledgment of their enthusiasm. When the Edisons attended the Paris Opera, the orchestra played "The Star-Spangled Banner." They were invited to watch the performance from the prompter's box.

They had lunch with Alexandre Eiffel near the top of his masterpiece, the Eiffel Tower. They visited Louis Pasteur at his medical laboratory and watched him innoculate a boy who had been bitten by a rabid dog.

All this impressed Mina Edison more than it did Thomas Alva Edison. She enjoyed the social whirl among celebrities. He disliked so much attention. Edison preferred the seclusion of their hotel room, where he could relax. Besides, his deafness created a problem when, as often happened, he got separated from his wife. And, finally, he felt so uncomfortable when speaking to crowds, or even to small groups, that he avoided these occasions whenever he could.

From Paris the Edisons went to Berlin. There they met, among other notables, the great German scientist Hermann von Helmholtz. Since Helmholtz had published a number of works on sound waves, and since Edison had used his discoveries while perfecting the phonograph, the two had much to say to each other.

The Edisons left Germany for England, where Edison saw the station at Holborn in London still operating as he had designed it in 1882.

And then the Edisons were on their way back to the United States. They arrived home on October 6, 1889. Edison was ready to get back to his laboratory research.

Making Movies

Edison eagerly returned to his West Orange laboratory after his European trip. He plunged into research on the third of his three greatest inventions. After the phonograph and the electric light bulb came the motion-picture camera.

Edison explained how he got the idea: "I had been working for several years on my experiments for recording and reproducing sounds, and the thought occurred to me that it should be possible to devise an apparatus to do for the eye what the phonograph was designed to do for the ear."

The problem was to capture motion by using a series of photographs. Still photography presented no problem. Many photographers were at work. Earlier in the century, Louis Daguerre of France had perfected the daguerreotype (1839), the best photographic process of its time. His still photos were achieved by a copper plate coated with silver oxide, sprayed with mercury vapor, and soaked in a salt solution. This technique was widely imitated. But how could motionless photographs record moving things?

"I had only one fact to guide me at all," Edison explained. "This was the principle of optics technically called 'the persistence of vision,' which proves that the sensation of light lingers in the brain for anywhere from one-tenth to one-twentieth of a second after the light itself has disappeared from the sight of the eye."

Persistence of vision is a familiar phenomenon that nearly everyone has experienced. Thus, if a wheel revolves very rapidly, the individual spokes stop being visible. The whole area inside the rim looks solid. The spokes are still there. But persistence of vision from spoke to spoke creates the illusion of solidity. Another example is a pad, the pages of which show a picture slightly varied from page to page. If all the pages are flipped rapidly one after the other, there is an illusion of movement. A horse will seem to be running, a dancer dancing, and so on.

Edison was not the first to think that persistence of vision might be the clue to motion pictures. He knew the work of earlier experimenters, particularly in England, France, Belgium, and Austria. He saw where and why they had succeeded and failed. He learned from their successes and failures.

The photographer whose work helped Edison most was Eadweard Muybridge. This English photographer developed a method of adding still photographs together that almost resembled a motion picture.

In 1872 Muybridge was hired to settle a wager between two wealthy California railroad owners. Leland Stanford bet Collis P. Huntington $25,000 that a running horse at one period in its stride has all four feet off the ground. Muybridge settled the bet by rigging up a series of twelve cameras, each with a thread attached. The threads were stretched across the race course where the experiment took place. As the running horse snapped the threads, one after another, the camera shutters were tripped. In this way, Muybridge got a series of stop-action photographs at very close intervals. These stills proved that sometimes the horse had all four feet clear off the ground. Muybridge successfully demonstrated that there is a gap between what the mind thinks it sees and what the eye actually perceives.

Muybridge went from this success into research on motion pictures. Étienne Marey was carrying out the same kind of research in France. Both achieved the illusion of motion through still photographs, but neither was able to solve the problem of how to do it with a single camera. William Friese-Greene of London had invented a motion-picture camera. He patented it in 1890. Friese-Greene wrote to Edison suggesting that it be combined with Edison's phonograph to produce talking pictures. Edison did not follow this suggestion because he already was experimenting with the phonograph and his own camera.

Edison's chief assistant on the project was William K.L. Dickson. He had come from London to work in the Edison laboratory. The two men worked together on many projects, most of them involving motion pictures.

The work was so intricate that failures were frequent. Edison pointed out, "We were dealing always with minute [tiny] fractions of a second." Today's scientists have instruments that can measure much smaller time periods. But in Edison's time, most of the scientific measuring had to be done by hand. That meant that there was the danger of failure if the photograph frames were not moved fast enough.

Help came from Rochester, New York. George Eastman had invented celluloid film, which was light, strong, and pliant. The film could be rolled up on a spool. Edison saw the meaning of Eastman's invention for motion pictures. A series of stills on a spool of film could be spun rapidly enough to trick the eye and give the illusion of movement. Edison adopted this film, abandoning the photographic plates then in use.

Edison experimented with all kinds of mechanisms before he came up with the best combination of lenses, sprockets, and lighting. He and Dickson tested the machine over and over again. Dickson described a remarkable scene: "On exhibition evenings the projecting room, which is situated in the upper story of the photographic department, is hung with black, in order to prevent any reflection from the circle of light emanating [coming out] from the screen at the other end, the projector being placed behind a curtain, also of black, and provided with a single peep-hole for the accommodation of the lens. The effect of these somber draperies, and the weird accompanying monotone of the electric motor attached to the projector, are horribly impressive; and one's sense of the supernatural is heightened when a figure suddenly springs into his path, acting and talking and then mysteriously vanishing."

Full-scale motion pictures required two things. First, a camera was needed to take pictures. Second, a projector was needed to reproduce and present them for viewing. Edison's camera was his Kinetograph (from the Greek meaning "moving writing"). His projector was his Kinetoscope ("moving view").

The Kinetograph is the mechanism associated with the early film industry when cameramen cranked their cameras by hand. Inside, the crank unrolled the celluloid film, which recorded the scene being played.

The film to be viewed was placed on a spool in the boxlike Kinetoscope. The film was held in place on the spool by sprockets, the teeth of which matched holes along the two edges of the film. A magnifying lens enlarged each still photo as it came into view. Edison chose 35mm film as the best width. His choice was so shrewd that this width remained standard in the movie industry until 1952. During the 1950s, wide-screen motion pictures arrived with Cinerama.

Edison's first motion-picture camera, the Kinetograph.

Edison took out his patent in 1891. Three years later he established the first of his "Kinetoscope parlors." These were places where the public could insert a coin and view through a peephole a short motion picture. Such movies were perhaps a half-minute of an acrobat tumbling or a horseman taking a jump. It was a dramatic experience for those who had never seen any kind of motion picture before. Edison's Kinetoscope parlor was the birthplace of the movie industry.

Edison's invention was taken up at home and abroad by inventors who improved upon it.

Thomas Armat, an American, produced the Vitascope in 1896. In early movies, actors' movements often were unnaturally rapid because the film moved too quickly between frames. The Vitascope had a mechanism that allowed single picture frames to remain in view a longer time without interrupting the flow of movement on the film. Viewers had more time to take in the contents of each frame without jerkiness from one frame to another. The Vitascope was such a good idea that Edison joined Armat in a partnership to manufacture it. The partnership lasted about a year. It ended after a dispute between the two inventors. Edison went ahead on his own.

In France the Lumière brothers, Louis and Auguste, controlled the speed of the frames by using a claw-like mechanism to move the film (1896). Their great contribution was to abandon the peephole system of viewing movies. They projected their film onto a wall screen. This is the system we still use today.

Many other inventors contributed to motion pictures as we know them. They developed new cameras and projectors.

Meanwhile, Edison was continuing with the making of motion pictures. The first movie studio was the one he built at West Orange—his Black Maria (named after a patrol wagon). The Black Maria, finished in 1893, was an ungainly structure. Edison explained: "Our studio was almost as amazing as the pictures we made in it. We were looking for service, not art. The building itself was about twenty-five by thirty feet in dimensions, and we gave a grotesque effect to the roof by slanting it up in a hunch in the center and arranging shutters that could be opened or closed with a pulley to obtain the greatest benefit from the light.

"Then, in order to make certain of as long a day as possible, we swung the whole building on pivots, like an old-fashioned river bridge, so it could be turned to follow the course of the sun. We covered it with tar paper, and painted it a dead black inside to bring our actors into sharpest relief. It was a ghastly proposition for a stranger daring enough to brave its mysteries—especially when it began to turn like a ship in a gale. But we managed to make pictures there. And, after all, that was the real test."

The first motion picture copyrighted in the United States featured Frederick P. Ott in *Edison Kinetoscopic Record of a Sneeze, January 7, 1894*. How Fred Ott was able to sneeze for the camera at just the right moment was not explained. One might well suspect that this sequence was simulated, that is, play-acted.

Edison made a prediction in 1894: "The kinetoscope is only a small model illustrating the present stage of progress, but with each succeeding month new possibilities are brought forth. I believe that in coming years, by my own work and that of Dickson, Marey, Muybridge, and others who will doubtless enter the field, grand opera can be given at the Metropolitan Opera House at New York without any material change from the original, and with artists and

The Black Maria, Edison's movie studio, was completed in 1893 in West Orange, New Jersey.

musicians long dead."

This prophecy has been fulfilled. We can see reruns of *Live from the Met* on television.

Edison went after big names to popularize his movies. William "Buffalo Bill" Cody came in his buckskins, boots, and beaver hat. His Wild West Show was famous in America and Europe. He performed for Edison's camera, waving his rifle with which he shot bison on the Great Plains.

The legendary strong man of the nineties, Eugene Sandow, displayed his muscular biceps before the camera. He went into his act of lifting heavy weights, bending iron bars, and tearing closed books with his bare hands.

James J. Corbett, then heavyweight champion of the world, put on a boxing exhibition in the Black Maria, which he did not find at all to his taste: "The Black Maria certainly did not look like an old-fashioned police patrol wagon. We hadn't been inside very long before most of us would have preferred a police patrol at that—for the little moveable studio was the hottest, most cramped place I have ever known."

Not all of Edison's motion pictures were filmed in this stifling environment. He also took his camera outside. One sequence was an imaginary battle scene from the Boer War in South Africa (1899).

A vital step forward in the art of motion pictures was to introduce a story. The first of this type filmed in the Black Maria was *The Life of an American Fireman* (1903). The first hit with the public was *The Great Train Robbery* (1904). Edwin S. Porter, Edison's associate, was the director of this classic film.

Films were silent until 1927, when Al Jolson appeared in *The Jazz Singer*. Movie audiences heard the human voice for the first time in a full-length film. This intrigued Edison. He had begun with the idea that his movies would be "talkies." He wanted to combine the phonograph and the camera. But this worked only for short films, and the sound kept slipping behind the picture, or vice versa. True talkies had to wait for a new technique. Bell Telephone developed a method by which a record player was mechanically adjusted to the camera.

Edison foresaw the time when motion pictures would become much more than merely entertainment. He realized that nonfiction would appeal to audiences in the form of newsreels and documentaries. So would travelogues, motion pictures about travel. He looked forward to a time when schoolchildren would learn their subjects by viewing films as well as by reading books. Disappointment that educators did not grasp this point was a basic reason why he dropped motion pictures: "When the industry began to specialize as a big amusement proposition, I quit the game as an active producer.

"A good many people seemed to wonder why I did so—maybe they still wonder. But the answer is simple enough. I was an inventor—an experimenter. I wasn't a theatrical producer. And I had no ambitions to become one.

"If, on the other hand, the educational uses of the camera had come more to the front, as I had hoped, and I had seen an opportunity to develop some new ideas along those lines, my story as a producer might have been very different. I should have been far more interested in going on."

Edison did not complain about this disappointment. In his usual fashion, he turned to other things that appeared promising to him.

Rocks and Rays

Edison always had a number of projects underway at the same time in his West Orange industrial complex. He could pick and choose from among them at any time for the one on which he wanted to concentrate. His choice might be the project that seemed nearest to success or that required his personal attention because his assistants were stuck or that stirred his curiosity or that promised the highest financial reward.

From 1891 to 1897 Edison gave much of his time to a project for recovering iron ore from the ground. Iron ore was in great demand for the manufacture of steel. Edison wanted to get into the business of providing iron ore for his generators and selling the rest to the steel companies.

This idea resulted in an Edison enterprise that failed. He started out in high hopes of success. He put six years into a determined effort to make his iron-ore enterprise pay its way. He spent a fortune. And finally he had to give up.

This iron-ore undertaking placed Edison under great personal stress and strain. It was a test of his character. He passed the test by struggling against tremendous obstacles and repeated disappointments.

Edison began by having a study made of iron-ore regions in the eastern United States. The study revealed that low-grade iron ore—ore having a low percentage of iron to a large percentage of rock—was to be found in the highlands of northwest New Jersey near the Delaware River. Edison purchased 19,000 acres and set up a company town (called Edison) where his workers could live. He built a company store where they could shop, housed them in wooden cottages, and provided them with water and electricity.

Edison brought in giant machines to handle the iron ore. Steam shovels dug out the rocks. Cranes loaded the rocks into cars pulled by engines. Rock crushers turned huge boulders into powder for the refinery.

The process began when Edison's engineers bored deep holes into the earth. The holes were filled with dynamite, which, when touched off, hurled thousands of tons of rock into the air. It seemed as if rocks were continually flying around because the crushers also tossed fragments upward. The crushers had massive rolls—solid iron wheels— revolving toward one another. The rocks that dropped between the rolls were crushed into powder. The powder then dropped onto a conveyor belt underneath. But the tops of the rocks frequently rebounded into the air when hit by the rolls.

It was dangerous work that caused injuries and even several deaths. Some men on the job were hit by flying rocks, got caught in the machines, fell from ladders, or suffered other accidents. So much strenuous activity was necessary because the highlands held only low-grade ore.

The fact that he had to work with low-grade ore did not discourage Edison. He had developed an invention to retrieve the ore from the rock. His invention was an ore separator. It was made up of a container holding powdered iron-bearing rocks, a dividing partition just below the container, and a magnet to one side of the partition. As the powder was released from the container and fell downward, the magnet pulled the iron granules, deflecting them to its side of the partition. The pure rock powder, not being affected by magnetism, fell straight down on the opposite side. The iron granules were then carried to the smelter, where they were heated, melted, and turned into iron ingots. These were blocks of iron that could easily be packed and shipped by railroad.

Edison succeeded in extracting iron from the low-grade ore of New Jersey's highlands, but the process was very costly. He even sold his stock in General Electric to raise funds. He might have had a profitable business eventually if it had not been for an unforeseeable development. High-grade iron ore was discovered in Minnesota's Mesabi Range. This ore reached the steel mills through a transportation system controlled by financial tycoon John D. Rockefeller. While Edison had to work hard to extract little iron from much rock, Rockefeller quite easily removed much iron from less rock. Rockefeller was able to make iron ingots cheaply and to sell them cheaply. Edison could not compete. In 1899 he ended his iron-ore business, saying: "Well, we might as well blow the whistle and close up shop."

He had lost a large sum of money, including the profits he would have made from the General Electric stock if he had not sold it at a low figure. He mentioned this point to his assistant, Walter Mallory:

Edison: "What would my stock be worth now?"

Mallory: "Over four million dollars."

Edison: "Well, it's all gone, but we had a heck of a lot of fun spending it."

The time Edison spent refining iron ore was not a total loss. Now he applied his experience to the manufacture of cement. He founded the Edison Portland Cement Company. He set up his plant in eastern Pennsylvania. There the earth held the limestone rock he needed. To handle it, he brought in rock crushers from his property in the New Jersey highlands. He designed the cement plant himself.

Edison's machines were bigger and more powerful than those used by his competitors. The machines could therefore handle bigger, heavier rocks. When the limestone was ground to powder, the powder went into kilns, special ovens, designed by Edison. The standard kiln was less than 100 feet long. Edison extended his to 150 feet. His competitors predicted that his kilns were too long and would twist and buckle under the heat. Edison proved they were wrong by developing a material capable of withstanding the stress. Soon his competitors were imitating him.

Another reason for Edison's success had to do with the cement itself. His cement was ground more finely than any other on the market. It was therefore easier to pour when wet. It also solidified more tightly as it dried, providing a stronger building material.

Soon Edison's company was producing more than a thousand barrels of cement a day, five times more than most of his competitors. He had customers for his entire production. Many were builders who were erecting tall structures of concrete reinforced with steel.

One of these structures was a marvel of its time—Yankee Stadium in New York City. When Babe Ruth was the home-run king of major-league baseball, fans began coming in droves to see Ruth play—so many that a new ballpark was needed to hold them all. Yankee Stadium arose. Opened in 1923, it was known as "the house that Ruth built." It might also have been called "the house that Edison built," because 180,000 bags of Edison's cement went into this famous ballpark.

But Edison also was interested in smaller buildings. He saw a market in helping ordinary families own their own homes. The houses would be less expensive than those on the market because they would be prefabricated, or constructed in standard sections, instead of being built piece by piece on their sites. They also would be cheaper because they would be mass-produced. Roof, walls, floors, and interior partitions dividing the rooms would be put together at the same time. Utilities such as heat, water, and electricity would be added later.

Edison did what would now be called a cost analysis. "A decent house of six rooms, so far as the shell would go," he estimated, "would cost only three hundred dollars."

In 1908 Edison took out a patent for a house made of cement. His plan was to construct iron molds into which wet cement would be poured on building sites. When the cement hardened, the molds would be removed, and the shell of the house would stand ready for use. The molds could be used over and over again in this process of mass prefabrication.

Edison, for all the thought and work on this project, never went into the low-cost housing business. He did not find enough interest at the time. His other inventions were demanding too much of his attention. Moreover, he hoped somebody else would pick up his idea of prefabricated cement houses. This may have been prevented by shattering national and international events of the early twentieth century.

World War I broke out in 1914 and lasted until 1918. The Great Depression began in 1929 and haunted the 1930s. World War II overshadowed the years between 1939 and 1945. When prefabricated housing became a booming industry, around 1950, new materials and new techniques had been developed. The idea of cement house frames became obsolete.

Edison still deserves credit for launching the idea of inexpensive prefabricated houses. As for his cement business, it made money and allowed him to pay off bills left over from his iron-ore venture.

Since Edison had a habit of working on a number of projects at the same time, some that started earlier than others ended later. Thus, his invention of the fluoroscope fell in the middle of his iron-ore venture. But the idea for the fluoroscope began much earlier, in the year 1895.

In that year, Wilhelm Roentgen, a German scientist, discovered X rays. Roentgen revealed to the world that X rays could pass through the body and leave shadows on a plate from which medical diagnoses could be made.

When Edison read of this discovery, he began experimenting with X rays. He tested many substances to see which formed the best screen on which to examine the shadows. This substance proved to be tungstate of calcium. He used it in constructing a machine with an eyepiece at one end and a screen at the other. Placing his hand between the screen and the source of the X rays, he squinted through the eyepiece. He saw the bones of his hand clearly etched on the screen.

Edison called his invention a fluoroscope. Foreseeing its importance in medicine, he rejected the idea of taking out a patent. Had he gone to the United States Patent Office in Washington, D.C., and asked for his fluoroscope to be recorded in his name, the lengthy process would have held up its use in hospitals. Edison's desire to help humanity would not allow him to delay the use of his invention. He was pleased when he learned from Professor Michael Pupin of Columbia University that the first x-ray operation in the United States was performed with the Edison fluoroscope.

In 1896 Edison had an interesting encounter with an inventor whose name would one day be as famous as his own—Henry Ford.

Ford worked for the Edison Illuminating Company in Detroit, where he had been for five years. During those years, Ford rose to be the chief engineer at the company's powerhouse. In 1896 he attended a meeting of the Association of Edison Illuminating Companies in New York. Ford had been an admirer of Edison for years and was very pleased to be introduced to Edison at this New York meeting. The two men had a long conversation while they sat next to each other.

Ford explained his ambitious plan for a car that would run on gasoline. Edison was impressed by Ford's idea. "Young man, that's the thing!" the older inventor exclaimed. "You have it—the self-contained unit carrying its own fuel with it! Keep at it!"

Ford did keep at it until he invented and built the car that transformed American life. He always appreciated the advice Edison gave him when he was developing the ideas that would make the automobile a reality.

In 1899 Edison began to work seriously on a problem that many inventors were working on. The problem was how to develop a practical storage battery. The ordinary battery had been known since the eighteenth century. Alessandro Volta had invented it. The difficulty was that this type of battery lost its energy when the source of power was cut off. The search in Edison's time was for a battery that would recharge itself. Inventors wanted to "store" electricity and keep it ready as needed.

Such a battery was invented before Edison's invention. It was largely the work of Camille Faure. This French inventor used a mixture of lead and sulphuric acid. Faure's invention worked. On the other hand, it was heavy and it leaked. The acid it contained ate into the parts and eventually ruined them. The theory was correct, but the practical application was not perfected.

Edison read up on what had been achieved with the storage battery and on what remained to be achieved. His verdict on the situation: "I guess I'll have to make a battery." He was in one of his moods—they came to him quite frequently—when he felt that the answer was out there waiting for him to discover it. He only had to work hard enough.

To R.H. Beach of General Electric, Edison said: "Beach, I don't think nature would be so unkind as to withhold the secret of a good non-acid storage battery if a real earnest hunt for it was made. I'm going to hunt."

He "hunted" in a manner that was second nature to him. He made countless experiments, testing all the substances that could conceivably give him his answer. He shook test tubes, mixed chemicals in basins, and frowned when the right results were not forthcoming. After each day's failure, he would hang up his chemist's gown and mask and do some more thinking about the problem.

Finally, through his experiments, the answer was found. The secret combination was iron, nickel, and potassium hydroxide. He built and sold a number of batteries—only to be faced with what looked like a disaster. Some customers who bought his batteries reported basic defects, such as leakage.

Edison never hesitated. He recalled his batteries, stopped producing more, and began a campaign to clear up the defects. He redesigned the battery and tested it until he was satisfied. Then he began selling his product again. This time his customers were satisfied.

Edison's storage battery was applied in many ways. One of those ways improved conditions in coal mines. The miners worked deep underground in dangerous circumstances. Their situation could be improved if they had better lighting.

Edison responded with a new type of miner's light. He adapted his storage battery when he made this invention. A small version of his battery was attached to a miner's belt. A wire was then extended from the battery to a lamp on the miner's cap. Thus a ray of light illuminated the area in which the miner was working no matter which way he turned his head. The mines became safer than they had ever been before.

Edison took out his patent for the miner's light in 1914. Everything seemed to be going smoothly at West Orange when suddenly a catastrophe struck. On December 9 a fire broke out in one of the buildings and spread to neighboring structures. The fire squad of the industrial complex could not control the blaze. Fire engines raced to the scene from nearby towns. Firemen brought out their hoses, axes, and scaling ladders. They attacked the blaze with everything they had. But their efforts were hampered by low water pressure.

The fire turned into an inferno because the buildings held so many chemicals, film, and other flammable substances. Even buildings of reinforced concrete were engulfed in flames.

Edison was at home in Glenmont when the fire started. He rushed to the scene, where he watched much of his West Orange plant go up in smoke. The central laboratory survived, but most of the buildings near it were destroyed.

The fire raged all night, and in the morning Edison stared at mounds of smoldering ashes. His staff and his friends in West Orange wondered whether the destruction would mean the end of Edison, the inventor.

That question never occurred to Edison himself. "I'm sixty-seven," he said, "but I'm not too old to make a fresh start."

The fresh start began immediately. He brought in a team to clean up the debris. With the ground cleared, he supervised the construction that enabled him to replace the lost buildings. And his West Orange plant rose from the ashes. By the beginning of 1915 Edison was back in business.

Edison was able to do this because he had remained hale and hearty. His hair had turned white, there were lines in his face, and he walked more slowly than in the past, but his mind was as busy as ever with plans for new inventions. He supervised his staff with all his old energy.

Far from being finished in 1914, Edison had seventeen years of work ahead of him.

CHAPTER

A Patriot in World War I

It was fortunate that Edison was mentally alert and physically active in 1914 because the United States needed him. That was the year World War I broke out. Edison would be in the thick of the American war effort until peace came.

On July 28, 1914, the Archduke of Austria and his wife were assassinated by a Serbian nationalist at Sarajevo, now in Yugoslavia but then in the Austrian province of Bosnia. This crime caused a chain reaction that drew all the major powers of Europe into a shattering collision.

Austria declared war on Serbia. Russia, Serbia's ally, mobilized its army and threatened Austria. Germany, Austria's ally, declared war on Russia. Germany also declared war on France, Russia's ally. Great Britain, France's ally, declared war on Germany.

The United States, under President Woodrow Wilson, remained neutral. Edison supported this policy. He was a humanitarian who opposed war as a method of settling international disputes. Nor could he see at the start of World War I that the Allies (Britain, France, and Russia) were any better than the Central Powers (Germany and Austria).

Questioned by a reporter about the war in Europe, Edison replied: "This war had to come. Those military gangs in Europe piled up armaments until something had to break."

As the war went on, Edison changed his mind. One jarring event for him, as for millions of other Americans, was the sinking of the *Lusitania* in 1915. A German U-boat (submarine) torpedoed the British ocean liner, sending it to the bottom of the sea, off the coast of Ireland. More than one thousand people died, including more than one hundred Americans.

The *Lusitania* incident shocked the United States into preparing for war. The U.S. Army and Navy were strengthened. Civilians were called on to do their bit for the national defense.

Edison was so famous as an inventor that the secretary of the navy, Josephus Daniels, approached him directly. Daniels was engaged in a crash program to increase American naval power. He wanted Edison to work on inventions that would be useful if ships of the U.S. Navy went into battle against German U-boats in the Atlantic.

In his autobiography, Daniels explained what he had in mind in 1915: "In that same year I wrote Edison that 'the imperative [all-important] need of the Navy is the utilization [use] of American genius to meet the new conditions of war,' and asked him to render 'a very great service' by organizing the inventive genius of the country. He responded patriotically and soon the Navy had Edison and 100,000 more inventors and scientists seeking new ways to win a new type of war. The story of what Edison and his associates did is a great chapter in naval history."

Actually, it was Edison's idea to round up so many experts. Daniels's first plan concentrated on big names, such as Edison and Orville Wright of aviation fame. Edison, on the contrary, suggested asking scientific organizations for the names of *all* who could be helpful in Washington, D.C. That was how the list of Edison's colleagues was drawn up.

Before taking up his duties in Washington, D.C., Edison made a trip to the West Coast for Edison Day at the San Francisco Exposition. Henry Ford, now a household name because of his automobile, and Harvey Firestone, owner of rubber plantations and the huge tire industry, went with him. They took the time to visit Luther Burbank, known for his experiments with plants and the development of new varieties by grafting stems of one plant onto another. Burbank's method of selecting one favorable plant out of many for further experiments caused Edison to comment that this was similar to his own method of choosing between chemical samples. Edison, too, kept the most favorable samples for further experiments.

Returning to the East Coast, Edison went to Washington, D.C., for the first meeting of what Daniels called "the Edison Navy Consulting Board." The official name was Naval Consulting Board. Edison became its president. His deafness made it impossible for him to communicate easily with the other scientists and inventors. Yet he became the guiding spirit behind the whole enterprise. He used the same system as he did at the West Orange laboratory, proposing ideas, theories, and experiments to be tried out by his subordinates or by himself.

Edison had great admirers among the men brought to Washington, D.C., by Daniels to contribute their expertise to the Naval Consulting Board. Robert Millikan, who after World War I was awarded the Nobel Prize in physics, said he found in Edison an unusual combination of intelligence and modesty.

There were delays in establishing the Naval Consulting Board. Therefore Edison did not have to be in Washington, D.C., all the time as 1915 drew to a close. He spent much of his time back in West Orange. There he worked on projects he had left unfinished, and thought about the application of technology to the needs of the expanding navy.

By the end of 1915, trenches were cut into the earth across Europe from the Alps to the English Channel. Millions of men in the trenches faced one another across "no-man's-land," where hundreds of thousands of lives were being sacrificed by both sides in attempts to advance a few miles. Trench warfare became a byword for hopeless misery when the Western Front was quiet. Trench warfare meant bloodshed on a terrifying scale when battles broke out.

Ford believed he could arrange for an end to the war in 1915 by appealing to the humane feelings and common sense of the leaders of the nations involved. He said he wanted to "get the boys out of the trenches by Christmas."

To that end, Ford chartered a sea-going vessel. He called it his Peace Ship. He invited dignitaries from different walks of life to sail with him and to add their prestige to the mission when he talked with European statesmen. Those who went were mostly pacifists as anxious as Ford to see an end to the war. He relied on Rosika Schwimmer for advice. She was a Hungarian pacifist, very persuasive, who had brought the Peace Ship idea to Ford in the first place. A number of newsmen signed up in order to get the story.

Ford was anxious to have Edison aboard—his close friend, fellow humanitarian, and universally respected inventor. He traveled to West Orange to discuss the mission with Edison.

Edison had already committed himself to work for the navy. Of course, that work would be unnecessary if Ford's plan led to a speedy end to the war. But Edison did not think this would happen. He therefore refused to become a passenger on the Peace Ship.

Still he would support any scheme that might lead to an armistice in Europe. He therefore agreed to be on the dock when the Peace Ship sailed from New York. He allowed himself to be photographed there. He spoke in favor of Ford's mission and wished it success.

Just before lifting anchor, Ford said to Edison: "I'll give you a million dollars to come along!" But Edison did not need a million dollars, nor did he believe in the Peace Ship. He was not surprised that Ford never got to see any of the European leaders. They were too bent on winning the war to spend any time with an American they considered to be naive. Edison did, however, dislike the ridicule to which American newspapers subjected the Peace Ship. He felt it represented a noble, if hopeless, mission.

Edison pinned his faith on the military might of the United States. In 1916 he marched in a parade in New York amid rifle-carrying soldiers in uniform and unarmed civilians. He was so deaf that he could barely hear the blaring music. But he saw the waving flags and cheering crowds. They made him feel patriotic as he marched up Manhattan from Washington Square to Central Park.

The war had interrupted trade between the United

States and Europe. As a result, the United States could no longer count on chemicals from Europe. Edison began to manufacture some of them. Some chemicals he required for his batteries and other commercial products. But most went into explosives and other military necessities of the U.S. armed forces. For this purpose, he added to his West Orange production by maintaining factories at Silver Lake, New Jersey.

Edison's work for the navy did not leave him with a very high regard for naval officers. He thought they were too inclined to go by the book instead of striking out with venturesome new ideas. That was why he wanted only scientists and inventors at the postwar Naval Research Laboratory. He hoped naval officers would not be appointed.

This was one of Edison's mistakes. He did not see that the navy, like the army, had to rely on proven tactics. Nor did he realize that both did in fact use new ideas. The Naval Research Laboratory was established in 1920 under the control of naval officers. It fulfilled its tasks very well. But Edison was an inventor who could risk a thousand failures to achieve one success. He never stopped to consider that one failure by the armed forces could spell disaster.

Before the United States got into World War I, the presidential election of 1916 took place. Edison supported President Woodrow Wilson for a second term. His reasoning was twofold. In the first place, the United States was still at peace. In fact, the slogan of the Democratic party was "Vote for Wilson, he kept us out of war." In the second place, Wilson's policy was for American preparedness. The nation would not be caught off guard if war came.

In Washington, Edison worked with Josephus Daniels,

secretary of the navy, and with Franklin Delano Roosevelt, assistant secretary of the navy in World War I (and president of the United States in World War II). Daniels was very respectful of Edison: "I always called Mr. Edison 'Commodore' and Congress voted him a Distinguished Service Medal." The U.S. Navy no longer had the rank of commodore in its grades from ensign to admiral, but it remained a term of respect. That was how Daniels used it in addressing Edison.

World War I was now at a critical stage. The stalemate of trench warfare on the Western Front continued. But the Germans were stepping up their submarine campaign against Allied shipping in the Atlantic Ocean. More and more ships were being torpedoed and sunk as they tried to make the crossing to American ports and back. The submarines lay in wait in the open sea. They ambushed merchant vessels sailing in their direction.

The British were dependent on seaborne traffic to bring in the food supplies they needed. German submarines cut into this traffic so disastrously that there was danger that Britain might be starved into surrendering.

To meet the danger, the British developed anti-submarine measures. First they adopted the convoy system. This meant that ships would no longer sail by themselves. Thus British ships would no longer present tempting targets to U-boat commanders watching the surface of the ocean through their periscopes. Instead, merchant vessels would sail in groups protected by warships. The British also used powerful depth charges to blast U-boats deep down in the water.

Although the United States was not yet in the war, tensions between the United States and Germany were reaching a breaking point. Josephus Daniels, as secretary of the navy, was determined to see that his sailors and ships were ready for anything. He relied on Edison to devise new ways to combat the German threat in the Atlantic.

Daniels observed in his autobiography: "Mr. Edison gave his time, at Washington and in command of a ship in southern waters, to experiments, devoting himself mainly to work on the detecting of the submarine and to the quick turning of cargo boats."

Edison's first antisubmarine invention was a device that could detect torpedoes as soon as they were fired. The device recorded undersea shock waves caused by torpedoes and pinpointed the direction from which they were coming. The captain of a merchant vessel or warship could then try to move it out of the torpedo's path.

Edison's second invention was a device for turning a ship sideways as soon as the sound of a torpedo was recorded on board. The torpedo might then pass to one side of the ship, leaving it unharmed.

Edison wrote of these two inventions: "I was successful in both. I built a listening apparatus, and while my boat was in full speed, I could hear a torpedo the instant it was fired nearly two miles away. And with my turning device, a 5,000-ton cargo boat, fully loaded, going at full speed, was turned at right angles to her original course on an advance of 200 feet."

These two inventions were ready when the United States went to war in 1917. President Wilson felt compelled to ask Congress for a declaration of war on Germany because of the policy of unrestricted submarine warfare announced in Berlin, the German capital. Until then, neutral shipping had been allowed through British or French ports. Unrestricted submarine warfare meant that U-boat commanders had orders to sink all ships, no matter what flag they flew or where they were going.

This was virtually a declaration of war on the United States, whose ships would come under German fire whenever they ventured out onto the high seas.

Edison was ready when American warships began fighting German U-boats in the Atlantic. He continued with what he was already doing. He kept coming up with new ideas for the navy to use. He estimated that he added "about forty-five inventions" to the science of naval warfare.

Apart from the torpedo locator and the ship turner, Daniels thought that five Edison inventions deserved special mention:

1. Edison developed a sticky chemical that could be spread over the ocean surface where U-boats were known to be operating. When a periscope went up, the chemical would cover its lens, leaving the commander looking into a useless piece of equipment.

2. The loud-speaking telephone was an adaptation of the instrument Edison had experimented with years before. He raised the volume so that a conversation could be carried on even in the midst of a naval battle.

3. The glare eliminator made it possible for surface ships to see periscopes when sunlight was glancing off the water. Edison's invention, using dark film, reduced the sunlight and made the periscopes visible.

4. Using a mixture of petroleum jelly and zinc dust, Edison created a coating for guns on American

submarines. This coating protected the guns from damage by salt water.

5. The fire-prevention chemical silicate of soda made it possible to control fires. Ships were fueled by coal during World War I, and fires often broke out in the coal bins.

Daniels felt grateful to Edison for his contribution to the American war effort. So did President Wilson, who took the time to salute Edison on his seventieth birthday in 1917.

"I was an undergraduate at the university when his first inventions captured the imagination of the world. And ever since then I have retained the sense of magic, which what he did then created in my mind. He seems always to have been in the special confidence of Nature herself."

Edison refused to take more credit than he thought he deserved. He saw the contributions to the war effort made by other members of the Naval Consulting Board. He never underestimated them. He knew that Lee De Forest, soon to be called by some "the father of radio," added electronic listening devices to the navy's antisubmarine arsenal. Scientists and inventors now forgotten aroused Edison's admiration for their ability to solve problems presented to them by the navy.

That was why Edison refused the Distinguished Service Medal when it was offered to him after World War I. He would not accept a decoration that he thought should be awarded to a number of other men who had worked hard and effectively for their country at the Naval Consulting Board.

On the Road

During the war, Edison needed occasional relaxation from the hard work he was doing for the navy. He spent most of these days at home. But once in a while he went for long tours through the countryside with his friends. There were three whose company he particularly enjoyed.

One was Henry Ford, his old acquaintance who had "put America on wheels" and consulted Edison about new projects for the automobile industry.

The second friend was Harvey Firestone, the leading manufacturer of tires, partly because he made them for Ford's cars. At first auto tires had been made of solid rubber around steel rims. They transmitted every jolt in the road through the body of the car. As a result, the passengers felt every jolt, too. The Firestone Tire and Rubber Company produced pneumatic tires—tires filled with compressed air. Ford put them on his cars, and the Firestone Company became more profitable than it had ever been. Ford and Firestone became friendly. Ford introduced Firestone to Edison.

The third of Edison's special friends was John Burroughs, a naturalist. Burroughs loved tramping through the woods wherever he happened to be—in New England, the South, or the West. In 1903 he tramped through Yellowstone Park with President Theodore Roosevelt. Burroughs met Edison in Florida when the Edisons were staying in their winter home at Fort Myers.

In 1914 Edison, Ford, and Burroughs went for a drive along the Caloosahatchee River into the Everglades. They got out of the car and roamed through the subtropical mangrove swamps. Burroughs, the naturalist, knew more about the wildlife than did his companions. He led them through the saw grass to where alligators lurked in the water. He discovered the nesting area of the beautiful roseate spoonbills. He talked about the water moccasins and the cougars inhabiting the Everglades.

Edison enjoyed the experience. He agreed with Ford that they should do it again, and that they should ask Firestone to go with them. Ford liked the Fort Myers area so much that he bought an estate next to Edison's.

The opportunity to experience nature again came in 1916, in a very different part of the country. Edison was in West Orange at the time, and he headed north up the Hudson. Ford could not go along because he needed to attend to his automobile factory in Dearborn, Michigan. Firestone and Burroughs joined Edison.

The party went into the Adirondack Mountains. They tramped over rugged, rocky terrain left over from the Ice Age. They looked up at high peaks and down into deep gorges. They got near enough to waterfalls to be splashed. They tossed stones into dozens of rivers and ponds.

The animals they spotted were deer, lynxes, foxes, and badgers. They walked through acres of wildflowers. They crossed the Adirondacks into Vermont.

Edison usually sat in the front seat beside the driver of his car. He wanted to be where he could have the thrill of seeing everything that came into view. He got out every so often to break rocks with a geological hammer to see what they were made of.

The Edison-Firestone-Burroughs party was on the trail for ten days. After the three men returned home, Burroughs wrote a letter to Firestone about the trip. In it, the naturalist said of the inventor:

"It was a great pleasure to see Edison relax and turn vagabond so easily, sleeping in his clothes and dropping off to sleep like a baby....Do you remember with what boyish delight he would throw up his arms when he came upon some particularly striking view? I laugh when I think of the big car two girls were driving on a slippery street in Saranac...and when they put on the brakes suddenly, how the car suddenly changed ends and stopped, leaving the amazed girls looking up the street instead of down.

"Mr. Edison remarked: 'Organized matter sometimes behaves in a strange manner.'"

Edison and Burroughs talked at night in front of the fire. They discussed Edison's inventions and Burroughs's experiences in the woods. Thus each learned something from the other. Burroughs saw that a smoothly working machine—like the phonograph—has a beauty of its own. Edison was led by Burroughs to a better understanding of wildlife and its mysteries.

Why do birds migrate? Why do squirrels hoard nuts? Why do spiders weave webs? Burroughs was passionate about such questions. Much of his enthusiasm rubbed off on Edison. When Edison returned to his gardening amid the lush trees, bushes, and flowers of Fort Myers, he felt more in tune with nature.

After the 1916 tour, Edison had occasion to write about Burroughs and Ford. He said:

"Mr. Ford has asked me to write something to be placed in the cornerstone of his new bird fountain (at Fairlawn in Dearborn), which cornerstone is to be laid by that lover of nature, John Burroughs.

"I am greatly pleased to do so, because, while mankind appears to have been gradually drifting into an artificial life of merciless commercialism, there are still a few who have not been caught in the meshes of this frenzy, and who are still human, and enjoy the wonderful panorama of the mountains, the valleys and the plains, with their wonderful content of living things—and among these persons I am proud to know my two friends, John Burroughs and Henry Ford."

In 1918 Ford rejoined the touring party, and the four friends—Edison, Ford, Firestone, and Burroughs—made their longest trip. It was also the trip with the greatest number of cars. There were half a dozen cars driven by chauffeurs. One car carried tents that were pitched every night for the four leaders to sleep in. Another car was a mobile kitchen that served hot meals. Trucks filled with supplies—from binoculars to mosquito netting—took care of their needs. Of course, all the cars were Fords.

John Burroughs was used to living in the woods in primitive conditions. Edison might have been willing to try it. But Ford and Firestone both wanted to travel in comfort. They therefore arranged to make this outdoor trip in the easiest manner. They produced the cars and the luxuries for this remarkable caravan winding its way through the wilds of America.

Meeting in Pittsburgh at the joining together of the Allegheny and Monongahela rivers, the travelers headed south. They toured West Virginia, crossed Virginia, and entered North Carolina. They spent much of their time in the Tarheel State in the Great Smoky Mountains along the Tennessee border.

Driving over fertile black soil good for farming, they reached the foothills of the Great Smokies. They passed forests of laurel and dogwood, and miles of azaleas blowing in the wind. They spotted white-tailed deer. Burroughs pointed out the tracks of black bears. Foxes and raccoons were everywhere. So were grouse, turkeys, and songbirds.

At the top of the Great Smokies, they reached the areas of red spruce and rhododendron. Here rivers began in small trickles before rushing down the mountainsides in broadening streams.

Edison loved every minute of it. "He is a good camper-out," Burroughs commented. "He can rough it week in and week out, and be happy."

When they stopped for the night, Edison entertained Ford, Firestone, and Burroughs with tales of his younger days, before he became famous. He described what he had seen and heard as a tramp telegrapher. They also heard about the practical jokes he played with his inventions. There were, for example, the hidden phonographs that startled people who did not know where the voices were coming from.

Edison brought some books with him on this tour. Whenever he could snatch a few minutes to himself, he would settle into the back seat of his car for a bit of reading. He read a lot of poetry in this way.

He was the only one of the four who did any reading. Burroughs, in his spare time, made notes to be worked up into books and essays. Ford and Firestone discussed practical matters, such as the best way to use water power for industry.

All of them returned home feeling refreshed and ready to get back to work. They looked forward to further trips together. In 1919 they were again in New York and New England. In 1921 President Warren G. Harding replaced Burroughs (who died that year) on a trip into Maryland. The 1924 camping trip took the three millionaire vagabonds to Massachusetts. But Edison was losing interest, partly because Burroughs was no longer there. He, Ford, and Firestone stopped going into the woods together.

Edison visited General Electric in Schenectady in 1922. Not having been there in some time, he was amazed at its explosive growth. The plant now employed 18,000 workers, many more than at the time of his last visit. Steinmetz, his successor as the great name at General Electric, guided him around the laboratories.

Five years later, Edison retired officially from his management of the West Orange industrial complex. He turned control over to his son, Charles Edison. But he always kept in touch with West Orange while wintering at Fort Myers. And he was pleased to know that his famous laboratory continued to be a success under the direction of his son.

But this did not mean that Edison gave up the laboratory work to which he had become accustomed during more than half a century. He continued to be an experimenter and an inventor. He still used the West Orange laboratory when he was staying at Glenmont.

In 1927 the National Academy of Sciences admitted Edison as a member. This was an acknowledgment of his contributions to science—his discovery of the "etheric force" and the "Edison Effect." Edison did not just tinker with mechanisms or chemicals. True, he was an inventor rather than a scientist. But he never carried out experiments at random just to see what would happen. He controlled his research with hard thinking and good judgment about each experiment.

Henry Ford, the auto manufacturer (left); Thomas Edison (center); and Harvey Firestone, the tire manufacturer (right), at a lumber camp in Michigan.

Edison and his wife were now spending more and more of their time in Florida. They called their winter home Seminole Lodge because Seminole Indians were the original people of the Fort Myers area.

Seminole Lodge was a two-story building with tall doorways and windows. A wraparound porch circled the ground floor. In warm weather the doors and windows were left wide open to catch the breezes blowing off the Caloosahatchee River. In bad weather heavy shutters were closed over the windows to keep the rain out. This was a wise precaution because storms occasionally blew up the river from the Gulf of Mexico.

Many of the chairs of Seminole Lodge were made of wicker. This is light material, ideal for the warm Florida climate. Mina Edison chose the wallpaper, furniture, pictures, and flower decorations for the rooms. The living room was lined with bookshelves holding the volumes her husband read in his spare time.

Edison, who invented the first practical electric light bulb, handled the lighting of Seminole Lodge. He never needed an electrician if something went wrong with the wiring. He did the repairs himself. After all, nobody knew more about electric lighting than he did.

The grounds of Seminole Lodge were covered with tropical vegetation. Palm trees towered over the house. Bamboo grew in great clumps along the river. Spanish moss hung from branches on which mockingbirds perched. A banyan planted by Edison grew into a giant.

Edison did his work in the laboratory established at Seminole Lodge. Bottles holding chemicals and jars holding bits of plant fiber stood on the tables. Test tubes hung in racks to one side. Curved faucets dripped into basins where

Edison mixed his liquids and tested his fibers.

The laboratory office contained his desk, his work-bench, his technical books, and the cot on which he took catnaps.

Seminole Lodge can be seen today as it was in Edison's time because it is maintained as a memorial to him. Known as the Edison Winter Home, it is open to the public. Charles Edison added the museum, which is filled with Edison's inventions. One feature of the museum is the car presented to Edison in 1907 by Henry Ford.

In his Menlo Park and West Orange laboratories, Edison showed he was a master of machinery. In his Seminole Lodge laboratory, he showed he was a master of botany—the study of plants.

Edison carried out his experiments at Seminole Lodge in the hope of discovering a new form of rubber. The idea for this research went back to 1914, when he had visited Luther Burbank's plant farm in California. Henry Ford and Harvey Firestone had been with him. Ford was interested in a reliable market from which to obtain cheap rubber for the tires on his cars. Firestone was interested because he man-ufactured tires. Ford and Firestone asked Edison if he could invent an American form of rubber that would make it unnecessary to import rubber from abroad.

Edison replied he was willing to try. He would apply the methods so successful in his laboratory to the study of plants. He knew that Burbank had produced an astounding num-ber of varieties of fruits and vegetables—including new varieties of potatoes, apples, and peaches. Edison would seek a new variety of rubber.

He did not do so in 1914 because he was tied up with his work in West Orange. Then World War I came and delayed everything. But the war showed how rubber supplies could be cut off. Edison resolved that this would not happen again if he could help it.

He was ready to begin in 1927 when he turned the West Orange plant over to his son. The Edison Botanic Research Company was founded in 1927 with financial assistance from Ford and Firestone. Edison gathered a staff of experts and began experimenting with plants containing latex, the material of which rubber is made.

Wanting to make the United States self-sufficient in rubber, he brought in plants from all over the country. The best turned out to be goldenrod. It had a higher percentage of latex than any other.

Edison took seeds from many types of goldenrod and planted them. When the seeds sprouted, he set aside the most hopeful shoots and grafted them together. He thus crossbred two plants to bring out the best features of both. Crossbreeding thousands of plants in this way, Edison developed a goldenrod fourteen feet tall. It had a higher latex content than any goldenrod ever seen before.

Edison felt sure that one day he would plant acres of goldenrod, harvest the latex, and manufacture rubber. Mrs. Edison wrote: "Everything turned to rubber in the family. We talked rubber, thought rubber, dreamed rubber. Mr. Edison refused to let us do anything else."

For all his success in crossbreeding and growing goldenrod, the rubber was not as good as that from foreign sources. Then Edison fell ill with digestive problems in 1929. He was never again able to work as energetically as before.

Edison recovered sufficiently to make the prediction: "Give me five years and the United States will have a rubber crop." Unfortunately, he did not have five years to live, only two years. He never did solve the problem of making rubber as good as the best on the international market.

Edison had the consolation of knowing that his labor with his plants was not wasted. In 1930 he received his last patent—and it was for his development of goldenrod rubber.

The Final Celebration

The year 1929 marked the fiftieth anniversary of Edison's invention of the first practical electric light bulb—the one that stayed lighted for forty hours and became the prototype of the lighting system that transformed the world. Edison's assistants, friends, and admirers were determined to celebrate the anniversary with fitting pomp and circumstance.

Henry Ford became enthusiastic about the celebration. Ford had the appropriate place to hold it—his new reconstruction of Edison's famous Menlo Park complex. This was in Greenfield Village at Dearborn, Michigan, not far from Ford's car factory.

Ford devoted Greenfield Village to American life in earlier times. He wanted to copy the type of town he had known as a boy. And so he had Greenfield Village laid out with a village green, streets, sidewalks, and buildings. The buildings included a town hall, a church, a general store, a schoolhouse, a blacksmith's shop, and a post office.

Ford also built models of famous buildings. The center-piece was a model of Independence Hall in Philadelphia, where the Declaration of Independence was adopted on July 4, 1776.

Ford's Greenfield Village also had buildings associated with famous people—people like songwriter Stephen Foster, botanist Luther Burbank, and the Wright Brothers, who invented the airplane.

Ford added Edison's Menlo Park to his list. He bought the Menlo Park property on May 7, 1928. He then began a search for relics of the great days when Edison worked there. This was a difficult task because the buildings had fallen into disrepair. Much of the damage occurred when a chicken farmer occupied the land and lived in one of the buildings.

Ford sent in a team to look for everything he could use in reconstructing Menlo Park. The members of the team had entire buildings taken apart and shipped piece by piece to Dearborn. They collected the contents of the buildings. They dug into the soil around the buildings and retrieved such things as test tubes, light bulbs, electrical wire, and crucibles in which Edison had melted metals. They accepted items donated by individuals who possessed souvenirs of their time with Edison. His original electric locomotive was transported to Greenfield Village.

Ford spared no pains to make his reconstructed Menlo Park as authentic as possible. Seven carloads of topsoil were brought from the New Jersey site and spread over the Greenfield Village site. The names of the streets were repeated. The buildings were restored. Even the boarding-house in which many of Edison's assistants lived while they worked for him was set in its proper place. Ford filled the buildings with Edison's original equipment whenever he could. He used similar objects from other sources when the originals were not obtainable.

In reconstructing Menlo Park, Ford relied on the one surviving veteran of the old days with Edison—Francis Jehl. He located Jehl in Europe and persuaded him to return to the United States. Jehl contributed his memory of the architecture, the layout of the rooms, and the furnishings of the buildings in which he had worked many years before.

Ford added something new, an Edison Institute. Its function was to promote Edison's philosophy of hard thinking and hard work.

Reconstructed Menlo Park was ready in time for the fiftieth anniversary of Edison's invention of his electric light bulb. The occasion was called Light's Golden Jubilee. The date was October 21, 1929.

Ford invited Edison to attend as the star of the show. Edison and his wife arrived at Greenfield Village two days early. The inventor was astonished to see his old Menlo Park complex before his very eyes.

Ford escorted him through the complex. Edison saw the office where he had read and drawn up his plans, the laboratory in which he had carried out his experiments, the test tubes in which he had mixed his chemicals, and the workbenches where he had achieved his breakthroughs with the phonograph and the electric light bulb.

When Ford asked Edison how authentic the Menlo Park restoration was, the conversation went like this:

Edison: "Well, you've got it about ninety-nine and one-half percent right."

Ford: "What's the matter with the other one-half percent?"

In 1929 Francis Jehl and Thomas Edison recreated the scene showing the invention of the first practical electric light during celebrations honoring the fiftieth anniversary of that invention. Henry Ford had reconstructed Edison's Menlo Park complex in Greenfield Village at Dearborn, Michigan.

Edison (chuckling): "We never kept it this clean!"

President Herbert Hoover and the First Lady arrived to take part in the festivities. They were met at the train station by the Fords and the Edisons. The party then transferred to a small train of the type on which Edison had worked as a candy butcher, printer, and experimenter when he was a boy.

Edison's sense of humor got the best of him during this ride. He marched up and down the aisle crying his wares, just as he had done decades before on the run between Port Huron and Detroit. All those aboard the train laughed when Edison offered apples, sandwiches, and candy bars.

A host of other dignitaries arrived for the celebration, including Orville Wright and Madame Marie Curie, the discoverer of radium. In the restoration of his old laboratory, Edison recreated with Francis Jehl the scene when he perfected the electric light bulb back in 1879. He flipped a switch, and the lights went on in the restored Menlo Park at Greenfield Village.

Edison was the guest of honor at the party that followed. However, since he had been seriously ill a few months before, the excitement was too much for him. He did not want to go to the banquet. Mina Edison persuaded him to attend, and he received an enthusiastic welcome from the other guests. The clapping and cheering lasted for several minutes.

President Hoover led the list of speakers who praised Edison from the podium. Hoover emphasized Edison's great service to humanity in bringing electric lighting to the world.

Edison managed to make a reply in which he said: "This experience makes me realize as never before that Americans are sentimental. And this crowning event of Light's Golden

Jubilee fills me with gratitude. As to Henry Ford, words are inadequate to express my feelings. I can only say to you, that in the fullest and richest meaning of the term—he is my friend. Good night."

The effort to speak at this final celebration of his life exhausted Edison. He suffered a fainting spell and had to be helped to Ford's house. There the stricken inventor spent several days in bed. Finally he was well enough to go home to West Orange.

"I'm tired of all the glory," he said. "I want to get back to work."

He was pleased that his family doctor agreed. The doctor realized nothing invigorated Edison as much as thinking about new inventions. And Edison got better as his assistants came to Glenmont to consult him about their work in the West Orange laboratory.

He relaxed, as he had throughout his life, by reading. Frequently he went back to Tom Paine, the author who inspired the Patriots of the American Revolution with the pamphlet *Common Sense*. "These are the times that try men's souls," Paine wrote in 1776, calling on the Patriots to stand fast for freedom in spite of all hardships. Edison could not believe in a good life without freedom. The works of Tom Paine were therefore well-thumbed volumes in his library.

Every so often, Edison and his wife would get into the back seat of the car presented to them by Henry Ford, and their chauffeur would drive them around West Orange. Edison was becoming more feeble, but he still enjoyed the ride.

He fell ill late in the summer of 1931. It was a severe attack for a man of eighty-four. His deafness became worse. He could no longer leave the house to work in the laboratory

Thomas Edison on the lawn at Glenmont, West Orange, New Jersey, 1930, his home for forty-five years.

or ride in the car. The best he could do was sit in a chair gazing out the window at the trees and flowers of Glenmont.

When Henry Ford visited him for the last time, Edison roused himself long enough to discuss the cars coming off Ford's assembly line. Then Edison lost his strength and sank rapidly. His last words were spoken while he was sitting in a chair gazing out the window. He said to his wife: "It is very beautiful over there."

He clung to his life a few days longer and died on October 18, 1931, in his bedroom at Glenmont.

His passing was mourned throughout the country and abroad. Ordinary citizens dimmed the electric lights in their houses on the day of the funeral. This was a fitting tribute to the man who made electric lighting available to everyone.

What had Edison achieved? A Congressional Medal awarded to him in 1928 gives the answer in a few simple words. The inscription reads: "He illuminated the Path of Progress by His Inventions."

Edison had faith in human progress through increased understanding of the laws of nature. He never stopped striving for that understanding. "Show me a thoroughly satisfied man," he declared, "and I'll show you a failure." He was never thoroughly satisfied, and he was not a failure.

He was born in 1847 into a world of gaslights and still photography. He departed in 1931 from a world transformed by electric lights, motion pictures, and the phonograph. He himself worked this transformation with his inventions.

When he began his career, the typical inventor was an individual working alone. When Edison's career ended, another of his inventions—the industrial complex—was transforming research. Many inventors now worked together in laboratories on specific projects. Under Edison's leadership, industry was moving into the modern era.

Thomas Alva Edison followed a vision for most of his long life. He turned that vision into reality in the laboratory. He thus made a success of himself, and at the same time became a benefactor of humanity.

Important Dates

1847 Thomas Alva Edison is born on February 11 in Milan, Ohio, the son of Samuel and Nancy Edison.

1854 The Edison family moves to Port Huron, Michigan.

1859 Thomas Edison begins to sell newspapers and candy on the trains running between Port Huron and Detroit.

1862 Edison publishes the first newspaper ever printed aboard a moving train; he rescues the son of a telegrapher, who teaches him telegraphy.

1864–67 Edison works as a tramp telegrapher in states from Michigan to Lousiana.

1868 Edison gains his first patent, for his electrical vote recorder.

1869 Edison goes to New York; he invents the stock ticker.

1871 Edison marries Mary Stilwell.

1875 Edison discovers the "etheric force" (which leads Marconi to the invention of radio).

1876 Edison moves to Menlo Park, New Jersey; he and his assistants establish the first laboratory devoted to industrial research.

1877 Edison invents the phonograph.

1879 Edison invents the first practical incandescent electric light bulb; he gives a public demonstration by illuminating Menlo Park.

1882 Edison opens the first power and lighting station (in London, England).

1883 Edison discovers the "Edison Effect" (which leads to the science of electronics).

1884 Edison's first wife dies.

1886 Edison marries Mina Miller; they begin to spend their winters in their home at Fort Myers, Florida.

1887 Edison moves his laboratory to West Orange, New Jersey.

1891 Edison perfects his motion-picture camera.

1893 Edison begins shooting motion pictures in his Black Maria, the first film studio.

1896 Edison invents the practical fluoroscope, which enables surgeons to perform the first x-ray operation in the United States.

1901 Edison constructs his cement plant in New Jersey.

1903 Edison perfects long kilns (ovens) that produce superior cement.

1914 Edison's West Orange laboratory is destroyed by fire; he immediately begins to rebuild it.

1915 Edison becomes head of the Naval Consulting Board, and for the next three years works on inventions to help the U.S. Navy during World War I.

1927–29 Edison experiments with rubber at his Fort Myers laboratory.

1929 Edison attends celebrations on the fiftieth anniversary of his invention of his first practical electric light bulb.

1931 Edison dies on October 18 at his home in West Orange, New Jersey at age 84.

Bibliography

Conot, Robert. *A Streak of Luck*. New York: Seaview Books, 1979.

Hall of History. "The Edison Era: 1876–1892." *A Century of Progress: The General Electric Story, 1876–1978*. Schenectady, N.Y.: A Hall of History Publication, 1981.

Hutchings, David. *Edison at Work: The Thomas A. Edison Laboratory at West Orange, N.J.* New York: Hastings, 1969.

Josephson, Matthew. *Edison: A Biography*. New York: McGraw-Hill, 1959.

Palmer, Arthur J. *Edison: Inspiration to Youth*. Milan, Ohio: Edison Birthplace Association, 1928.

Runes, Dagobert D., ed. *The Diary and Sundry Observations of Thomas Alva Edison*. New York: Philosophical Library, 1948.

Index

About the Author

Vincent Buranelli holds an M.A. in political science from the National University of Ireland and a Ph.D. from Cambridge University. He is the author of ten books in history and biography, and of more than a dozen stories in the Hardy Boys series. He is the coauthor with his wife Nan of an encyclopedia of espionage. He lives in Edenton, North Carolina, and is working on a biography of the famous explorer David Livingston. He is a member of the Authors Guild.